Queer Theories: An Introduction

This is a short and accessible introduction to the complex and evolving debates around queer theories, advocating for their critical role in academia and society. The book traces the roots of queer theories and argues that Foucault owed an important debt to other European authors including the feminist and homosexual liberation movements of the 1960s–1970s and the anticolonial movements of the 1950s.

Going beyond a simple introduction to queer theories, this book situates them firmly in a European and Italian context to offer a crucial set of arguments in defence of LGBTQI+ rights, in defence of the freedom of teaching and research, and in defence of a radical idea of democracy. The narrative of the book is divided into three short chapters which can be read independently or in sequence. The first chapter argues that queer theories are rooted in the critical philosophical tradition, the second presents a critique of heterosexism and the binary inherent to the gender-sex-sexual orientation system, and the third chapter sketches a history of the queer debate. The book offers a useful typology of queer theories by sorting them into three basic paradigms: Freudo-Marxism, radical constructivism, and antisocial and affective theories, clarifying the complexities of the nature of the debates for undergraduates.

The book is both accessible and original, and is suitable for both specialist researchers and undergraduate students new to queer studies. It will be essential reading for those studying philosophy, sexuality studies and gender studies.

Lorenzo Bernini is Associate Professor of Political Philosophy at the University of Verona, Italy, where he founded the Research Centre PoliTeSse (Politics and Theories of Sexuality, www.politesse.it) which he now directs. He is also a founding member of GIFTS – the Italian network of Gender, Intersex, Feminist, Trans-feminist and Sexuality Studies (https://retegifts.wordpress.com/). His interests range from classical political philosophy (especially Thomas Hobbes) and French thought of the twentieth century (especially Michel Foucault), to contemporary theories of radical democracy, critical race theories and queer theories. Among his books: *Il sessuale politico: Freud con Marx, Fanon, Foucault* (Edizioni ETS, 2019); *Queer Apocalypses: Elements of Antisocial Theory* (Palgrave Macmillan, 2017), previously published in Italian (Edizioni ETS, 2013) and Spanish (Editorial EGALES, 2015); as well as the Italian publication (Edizioni ETS, 2017) and Spanish publication (Editorial EGALES, 2018) of this book.

Gender Insights

Queer Theories: An Introduction
From Mario Mieli to the Antisocial Turn
Lorenzo Bernini

Objectification
On the Difference Between Sex and Sexism
Feona Attwood, Alan McKee, John Mercer, Susanna Paasonen and Clarissa Smith

https://www.routledge.com/Gender-Insights/book-series/GendIn

Queer Theories: An Introduction

From Mario Mieli to the Antisocial Turn

Lorenzo Bernini

Translated by
Michela Baldo and Elena Basile

Routledge
Taylor & Francis Group

LONDON AND NEW YORK

First published 2021
by Routledge
2 Park Square, Milton Park, Abingdon, Oxon OX14 4RN
and by Routledge
52 Vanderbilt Avenue, New York, NY 10017

Routledge is an imprint of the Taylor & Francis Group, an informa business

Translated by Michela Baldo and Elena Basile

Published in Italian by Mimesis Edizioni 2017

British Library Cataloguing-in-Publication Data
A catalogue record for this book is available from the British Library

Library of Congress Cataloging-in-Publication Data
Names: Bernini, Lorenzo, 1973- author. | Bernini, Lorenzo, 1973- Teorie
queer. English.
Title: Queer theories: an introduction : from Mario Mieli to the antisocial
turn / Lorenzo Bernini ; translated by Michela Baldo and Elena Basile.
Other titles: Lectures. Selections
Description: Abingdon, Oxon ; New York, NY : Routledge, 2020. |
Originally published in Italian in 2017 by Mimesis as: Le teorie queer :
un'introduzione. | Includes bibliographical references and index.
Identifiers: LCCN 2020010999 (print) | LCCN 2020011000 (ebook) |
ISBN 9780367196486 (hardback) | ISBN 9780367196493 (paperback) |
ISBN 9780429203695 (ebook) | ISBN 9780429512117 (adobe pdf) |
ISBN 9780429515545 (epub) | ISBN 9780429518973 (mobi)
Subjects: LCSH: Sexual minorities. | Queer theory. | Gender identity. |
Sexual orientation.
Classification: LCC HQ73 .B47213 2020 (print) | LCC HQ73 (ebook) |
DDC 307.76--dc23
LC record available at https://lccn.loc.gov/2020010999
LC ebook record available at https://lccn.loc.gov/2020011000

ISBN: 978-0-367-19648-6 (hbk)
ISBN: 978-0-367-19649-3 (pbk)
ISBN: 978-0-429-20369-5 (ebk)

Typeset in Sabon
by Taylor & Francis Books

Contents

Acknowledgements

I warmly thank all the students of my courses at the University of Verona and at the University of Milan-Bicocca, who have contributed with their comments and criticism to the development of my reflections, and that every year give meaning to my academic work. Sincere thanks also to the Research Team of the centre PoliTeSse, all my friends from the Department of Human Sciences at the University of Verona, and the GIFTS network. I also wish to thank the 'mir' group, which organises the training course in 'Critical Theory of Society', in the book series of which the first edition of this book came out: Stefano Bracaletti, Giacomo Clemente, Didier Contadini, Luisa L. Corna, Lorenzo D'Angelo, Sara Maani, Vittorio Morfino, Michele Parodi, Luca Pinzolo, Gianluca Pozzoni, Stefano Sacchetti, Magda Taverna and Elia Zaru. My gratitude goes also to Massimo Prearo who discussed with me every page of this text, dispensing valuable advice. And finally, I thank Michela Baldo, Elena Basile, Adriana Cavarero and Mariano Croce, without whom this English edition would not have been possible.

Translators' preface

Le teorie queer di Lorenzo Bernini

Michela Baldo and Elena Basile

Translating Lorenzo Bernini's book *Le teorie queer* presented a series of linguistic and cultural challenges, which are inevitable for a book that, while firmly rooted in the Italian context, attempts to trace the transnational genealogies of different critical approaches to sexuality, which today loosely fit under the label of queer theories. In particular, Bernini's book engages in robust conversations with Italian, French and Anglo-American traditions of critical thought, tracing a number of important lateral connections, especially between French and Italian traditions, that are not always well served by existing English translations, or by assumptions of direct translational equivalence. This preface offers an extended list of the issues we encountered and an explanation of the choices we made. None of these were easy and we settled on them only after extended hours of research and vigorous conversations among ourselves and with Lorenzo Bernini, whom we thank for his patience, attention to detail and willingness to answer our questions. As it happens, the translational variations that inevitably attend to the transnational circulation of contemporary queer philosophies and politics can be as contentious as they are timely, and the choices we made in this English version of Bernini's book are no different. We hope this guide to the contextual reasons surrounding our choices will help the reader navigate the book with greater awareness of the inherent difficulties of translation as an art of crossing that contributes to the living transformation of languages and cultures through the very process through which it connects them.

'Sesso', 'binarismo sessuale' and gender pronouns

One of the first problems we encountered was the question of how to translate Bernini's use of the noun 'sesso' and the adjective 'sessuato', which in Italian tend to refer simultaneously to what, in the English tradition, are the more sharply delineated categories of 'sex' and 'gender'. Whereas in the Anglo-American feminist tradition the distinction between 'sex' and 'gender' (where sex belongs to biology and gender belongs to culture) is well established, in Italian feminist discourse it is less pronounced and thus 'sesso' may straddle both 'sex' (nature) and 'gender' (culture). This is because the concept of 'gender', understood in the Anglophone feminist tradition since the late 1960s as the social construction of sexual differences, was imported into Italian through translation only in the late 1980s (Di Cori, 1987). The term used for the translation was 'genere', a term which already existed in Italian to designate grammatical gender. However, according to Di Cori (1987), the acceptance of 'genere' as the best translation of gender proved difficult, not only because of the primarily grammatical meaning accorded to 'gender', but mostly because the term was perceived to be anonymous and not to recognise the historical specificity of women in the Italian intellectual scene. The Italian term 'sesso' [sex] is still prevalently used for both sex and gender and its use has been reinforced by the Italian feminism of sexual difference, which tended to use sex as a synonym for gender (see D'Amelia, 2000). Bernini uses 'sesso femminile' and 'sesso maschile' in this sense in Chapter 2, specifically in reference to Simone de Beauvoir and Luce Irigaray, who use the French 'femme' [woman] and 'homme' [man]. Our translation reflects current English translations of De Beauvoir and Irigaray ('woman' and 'man') and adds a translators' note explaining the connotational nuances of such terminological slippages between Italian, French and English.

The expression 'binarismo sessuale', which Bernini uses extensively in Chapter 2, also posed a series of problems. Eventually we chose to translate it with the expression 'sex/gender binary system', even though its immediate equivalent would be 'gender binarism'. The decision to underscore the fact that the binary is, indeed, a system that covers sex *and* gender simultaneously was motivated by two factors: one was the aforementioned tendency in Italian feminist discourse to use 'sesso' [sex] also to designate 'gender'; the second factor was the very topic of Chapter 2: the history of trans- and inter-sex activism, particularly in the Italian context. The expression 'sex/gender binary *system*' thus aims to avoid a potential ambiguity inherent in the simple expression 'sex/gender binary', which can be read to indicate the binary *between* sex and gender, rather than the idea that both sex and gender are binary constructs (female and male; femininity and masculinity). Thinkers in trans-gender studies, in particular, have contested a rigid feminist under-standing of the binary between sex and gender as having exclusionary effects on the sex and gender entanglements of intersex and trans people (see Hird, 2000).

Another translation choice we made in consultation with the author was in relation to the use of the generic personal pronoun. We decided to maintain a degree of historical accuracy when Ber-nini makes reference to philosophers such as Kant, by using the masculine personal pronoun to refer to the philosopher. In doing so, we kept Kant's male-centred grammatical choices, which were also shared by the majority of classical philosophers, as humanity for them is mainly represented by male human beings. Generally, how-ever, Bernini's and our own contemporary usage of personal pro-nouns strives to be as inclusive as possible, and the reader will frequently find the singular 'they' and 'them self' to signal the inclusion of a wide spectrum of gender identities against the exclu-sionary effects of binary gendered pronouns.

Translating Foucault: 'ontologie dell'attualità' and 'dispositivo di potere'

Bernini's frequent references to two major Foucaultian concepts – 'ontologie de l'actualité' and 'dispositif' – also proved challenging to translate, since the available English translations of both concepts do not capture the same nuances that Bernini draws attention to in his book, and which are prominent in the Italian translation of 'ontologie de l'actualité' as 'ontologia dell'attualità' and of 'dis-positif' as 'dispositivo'.

With regards to 'ontologie de l'actualité' (Foucault, 2008, p.22), the English published translation of Foucault's lectures translates this expression with 'ontologies of present reality' (Foucault, 2010, p.21), which does not capture the full semantic range neither of the French 'actualité', nor of 'attualità', the Italian translation that Bernini uses extensively. In a long email conversation with the author, we discussed the pros and cons of using the English word 'actuality' instead of 'present reality' to translate 'attualità'. While the English word 'actuality' has the advantage of recalling the philosophical dimension of 'attualità', which encompasses both the notion of 'present reality' and the more philosophical and dynamic idea of what becomes actual in the unfolding of events, it is very rarely used as a synonym for 'current times' or 'the present moment'. Eventually we decided to use the word 'actuality' to translate 'attualità', where Bernini highlights the philosophical concept of actuality as the dynamic actualisation of power through the subject and of the subject through power. Where the word 'attualità' refers more obviously to the concept of current events or current reality, we have opted to translate 'attualità' with 'the present', 'present reality', or 'current times'. Finally, where Bernini discusses Deleuze and Guattari's distinction between the 'actual' (Fr. 'actuel') and the 'present', the Italian 'attualità' has been rendered as 'the actual' (see Chapter 1).

As for 'dispositif', another crucial Foucaultian term that is foundational to Bernini's discussion of the specific power relations attending to the historical and contemporary regulations of sexuality, our options in English were fairly limited and none of them satisfactory. Initially we alternated between 'device', 'apparatus' and 'deployment' as acceptable choices, since all three renderings have been extensively used in the English translations of Foucault's works, with 'apparatus' in particular being used for the English translation of Agamben's major Italian commentary on Foucault's concept (see Agamben, 2009). However, since none of us, including the author, was satisfied with this patchy solution to the problem, we decided to dig a bit further into the history of 'dispositif's' translation into English. The difficulties attending to the English translation of the term were signalled in 2008 by Graham Burchell. In his 'Translator's Note' to Foucault's *Psychiatric Power: Lectures at the Collège de France 1973–1974*, Burchell writes that there 'does not seems to be a satisfactory English equivalent for the particular way in which Foucault uses this term to designate a configuration or arrangement of elements and forces ... that is both *strategic* and *technical*' (2008, p.xxiii). While Burchell opts to use 'apparatus', contemporary Foucaultian scholars have increasingly questioned such choice, particularly because it collapses a distinction that Foucault makes between 'appareil' (which is always translated as 'apparatus') and 'dispositif' (see Bussolini, 2010; Callewaert, 2017; Raffnsøe et al., 2014). These scholars make persuasive arguments for reintroducing the old English word 'dispositive' to translate 'dispositif'. In particular, Raffnsøe et al. (2014) argue that 'dispositive', despite being obsolete, is still a 'preferable' translation because 'it covers almost the same semantic field as the French word', since it includes a common etymological relation to the 'Latin verb *dis-pōnăre* [*sic*]' which means '"to set in order", "to arrange or array", "to dispose", or "to form"' (p.277). 'These older connotations of the word *dispositive*', Raffnsøe et al. tell us, 'are relevant for understanding its significance in Foucault's body of work' (p.277). Raffnsøe's and other scholars' explanation of the value of reintroducing the ancient English word to translate Foucault's 'dispositif', convinced us that 'dispositive' was the best way to translate Bernini's extensive use of Foucaultian expressions such as 'dispositivo di potere' ('dispositive of power') and 'dispositivo di sessualità' ('dispositive of sexuality'). We trust that the reader will appreciate this choice.

As the paragraph above indicates, our translation choices were frequently constrained by the available English translations or by the wording present in the English source texts of the corresponding works quoted in Italian translation by the author. Translating this work has thus involved extensive bibliographical research and frequent decisions regarding exactly which edition to use (and there were quite a few to choose from sometimes). The choice of which terminology to use has indeed entailed researching and reading a variety of articles or website entries on how philosophical concepts have been differently translated into English (and other languages) throughout history, according to any one author's preference for a specific nuance of the term or expression in question. Our translation practice was greatly enriched by learning about how the development of philosophical thought has been heavily influenced by these translation choices, and we are grateful to the translation scholars whose attention to such details offered us a wider range of options to choose from.

'Ideologia del gender' and 'famiglie naturali'

In Chapter 2 the reader will find frequent references to expressions such as 'ideologia del gender' [ideology of gender] and concepts such as 'la famiglia naturale' [the natural family]. We added two translators' notes in relation to these concepts, so as to elucidate further the political context of the Italian debate.

Specifically, we have drawn attention to the presence of an English borrowing in the Italian expression 'ideologia del gender' [ideology of gender]. This concept that has been used for about twenty years by the Catholic Church and by Italian Catholic-inspired conservative movements to indicate a caricatural version of feminist and queer theories. Notably, it contains the English loan-word 'gender'. The pointed use of an English word in the Italian phrase underscores the perceived foreignness of such concept and hence its perceived intrusion into an Italian culture to which, supposedly, it does not belong.

Another important debate, which is strictly linked to the ideology of gender, is one that involves the definition of the 'natural family' [famiglia naturale] and the discriminatory effects of such definition on the Italian legislation for same-sex couples. The term is very often used in discourses related to the ideology of gender, that stress how such ideology is meant to threaten the existence of the natural family, composed by a man and a woman, and thus based on compulsory heterosexuality and on the binary sex/gender system. In Chapter 2 Bernini points out that the conservative discourse surrounding the 'natural family' implicitly informs Italian legal discourse related to the rights of same-sex couples, who are currently legally deprived of the right to be called a family. Since the author is talking to an Italian audience familiar with 2016's civil union law regulating same-sex couples, we reproduced in a note the relevant section of the law that assigns to same-sex couples the legal designation of being 'a specific social formation', and thus not a family.

'Teorie queer'

In Chapter 3 Bernini delineates multiple genealogies for queer theories, in which he distinguishes between his own pre-dating of queer theories back to the work of Foucault, Mieli, Hocquenghem and 'le teorie queer propriamente dette' [properly named queer theories]. In short, 'teorie queer propriamente dette' in Bernini's book, is a phrase that refers to the collection of primarily North-American publications in English by authors such as Butler and Sedgwick (among many others), which between the 1990s and 2000s came to form the canonical backbone of academic research in the field of Queer Theory (wherein capitalisation and the use of 'Theory' as a collective noun signal the institutional sedimentation of such research). We thus decided to translate with 'Queer Theory' whenever Bernini refers to such body of work (primarily coming from the United States and primarily published between the 1990s and the 2000s) in contrast to the specific genealogy of *queer theories* (in the plural and in small caps) that Bernini himself is offering in the book.

Given Bernini's frequent emphasis on genealogical inquiry and on the specific historical moments of emergence of different queer theories, we found it necessary to insert the original dates of publication for works that are of historical significance in Bernini's argument. Hence readers will find some of the bibliographic references listed with two dates: the first one indicates the first date of publication, whereas the second date indicates the date of translation. While unusual, we hope that this way of listing some of the main references helps readers get a better sense of the historical timelines (and time *lags*) punctuating the circulation of foreign language texts in English.

In conclusion, this translation project has required us to navigate across the various understandings of queer theories by casting doubts, searching, reading, commenting, theorising, Skyping across continents (Europe and North America) and time zones and visiting physical and virtual libraries. Our translation practice can thus be understood, following Carol Maier (2006) as a practice of 'wondering and wandering' (p.163), wherein translation becomes its own kind of 'theoria', a practice, that is, that entails contemplation, wonder and metaphorical travelling. We trust that readers will carve their own queer and translative trajectories of wonder and travel along the paths the author has expertly guided us through.

Leicester and Toronto, 25 January 2020

References

Agamben, G. (2009) *What is an Apparatus? And Other Essays*. Translated by D. Kishik and S. Pedatella. Stanford: Stanford University Press.

Burchell, J. (2008) 'Translator's Note' in M. Foucault, *Psychiatric Power: Lectures at the Collège de France 1973–1974*. New York: Picador, pp.xxiii–xxiv.

Bussolini, J. (2010) 'What Is a Dispositive?' *Foucault Studies* 10: 85–107.

Callewaert, S. (2017) 'Foucault's Concept of Dispositif', *Praktiske Grunde. Nordisk tiksskrift for kultur* 1–2: 29–52.

D'Amelia, M. (2000) '"Genere" and "Sesso" in Italian Language and Feminism' in R. Braidotti and E. Vonk (eds), *The Making of European Women's Studies: A Work in Progress Report on Curriculum Development and Related Issues*. Utrecht: ATHENA, pp.83–89.

Di Cori, P. (1987) 'Dalla storia delle donne ad una storia di genere', *Rivista di storia contemporanea* 4: 548–559.

Foucault, M. (2008) *Le Gouvernement de soi et des autres: Cours au Collège de France. 1982–1983*. Paris: Seuil/Gallimard.

Foucault, M. (2010) 'Lecture of 5 January 1983' in F. Gros (ed.), *The Government of Self and Others. Lectures at the Collège de France 1982–1983*. Translated by G. Burchell. London: Palgrave Macmillan, pp.1–40.

Hird, Myra J. (2000) 'Gender's Nature: Intersexuality, Transsexualism and the Sex/Gender Binary', *Feminist Theory* 1(3): 347–364.

Maier, Carol (2006) 'The Translator as Theoros' in T. Hermans (ed.), *Translating Others*, vol. 1. Manchester: St. Jerome Publishing, pp.163–180.

Raffnsøe, S., Gudmand-Hòyer, M. and Thaning, M.S. (2014) 'Foucault's Dispositive: The Perspicacity of Dispositive Analytics in Organizational Research', *Organization* 23(2): 272–298.

Introduction

Studying queer theories in the Italian university

In the United Kingdom, the United States and other Anglophone countries, as well as in many Northern and Central European countries, gender and queer studies have long been included within the official academic canon. In contrast, in South America, Eastern Europe and Mediterranean Europe, they are scarcely present in academic curricula and are the object of ongoing political dispute. In Italy, in particular, these studies are not included in the official list of the academic disciplines of the Ministry of Education, University and Research, and those lecturers and researchers who carry them out do so within research programmes and courses that are named differently. For example, the module I teach for my MA degree course in Philosophy at the University of Verona is officially considered part of Political Philosophy, because I have been hired by the University of Verona as associate professor of Political Philosophy. However, with the consent of colleagues in the Philosophy programme, my module appears in the study plan with the name of 'Political Philosophy and Sexuality'. With the necessary clarifications, this name could well apply to the definition of queer theories that I propose in this book. The clarification pertains to the term 'philosophy', which I use in my courses, as well as in this book, to refer to the tradition of critical theory typical of continental European philosophy, and not to the analytical philosophy that prevails in American universities.

It takes, in short, some creativity and good negotiating skills to teach gender studies or queer theories in Italian universities. In recent decades, courses on Women's History, History of Homosexuality, Philosophy of Sexual Difference, Gender Studies, Gender and Sexuality, and many more, have appeared in many universities. Yet, these do not figure as official subjects, and are formally registered with more traditional denominations, such as History, Sociology, History of Philosophy, Political Philosophy or others. From the point of view of research, the situation is peculiar: academics are forced to rethink each time the epistemological status of what in English is called 'study' or 'theory'. If, then, we combine such an exercise in translation with an exercise in the history of thought – as will happen in this book – the results may be far from expected.

For academics working with queer theories in the United States, for example, it is now a cliché – and rightly so – to trace the origins of such theories back to the research on the history of sexuality carried out by Michel Foucault in France in the mid-1970s, and thus more or less fifteen years before the scholar of Italian background, Teresa de Lauretis, presented her famous paper on queer theory at the University of California, Santa Cruz. Less investigated is, however, the fact that Foucault's work owes much to that of other authors from Europe and its colonies. Some of them were academics, such as Hebert Marcuse, Simone de Beauvoir, Gilles Deleuze and Félix Guattari. Others were activist intellectuals, close to social movements, who were not always academic lecturers. One of the original aspects of this book, if compared to other general introductions of this kind, consists, I believe, in its emphasis both on the multiplicity of queer theories, which are, throughout this text, always referred to in the plural, and on the multiplicity of their possible genealogies. If some of these genealogies take us back to the University of California, to the Stonewall riots and to African-American feminism, others point to the European feminist and homosexual liberation movements of the 1960s and 1970s, and to the movements against colonialism of the 1950s, to authors, for example, such as the Italian Mario Mieli, the French Guy Hocquenghem and the Martinican Frantz Fanon.

Did we then really need another introduction to queer theories, written from continental Europe, from Southern Europe, from Italy, places which are generally considered as having imported these theories from the United States? I believe we do, and for different reasons, which I will attempt to explain via the following seven arguments.

1. Pedagogy. One of the reasons I wrote this book is connected to my academic work, which involves both doing research and teaching. Briefly, I thought that in Italy there was no textbook on queer theories, which would introduce queer theories to interested students and readers, without being limited to importing the American narrative on the topic. What was needed was a text that would reinstate the philosophical depth of these theories by taking into account the background of Foucault's thought.

The first edition of the book was published in 2017 as part of the book series 'Teoria critica della società' ['Critical Theory of Society'] by the Italian publisher Mimesis. The editors of the series are the organisers of the specialisation course by the same name at the University of Milan-Bicocca, where, since 2015, I have been teaching an intensive seminar in the title of which I was able to name queer theories, finally and explicitly. This book, more specifically, is an edited version of the lectures that I prepared for that seminar, and which constitute now the premise for the topics that I develop every year in my classes in Political Philosophy and Sexuality at the University of Verona. The book's origins, then, in a course dedicated to critical theory, explain its insistence on the critical character of queer theories.

In order to account for this critical aspect in the next pages, I won't present queer theories as a homogeneous corpus of thought, but I will describe them through their variety, as a lively debate that has been engaging with different ways of theorising the relationship (or juxtaposition) between politics and sexuality for at least half a century. As part of this debate I will outline three different paradigms or understandings of the sexual subject and its possibilities for political action, which I will respectively refer to as 'revolutionary Freudo-Marxism', 'radical constructivism' and 'antisocial theories'. I am aware that experts may consider this subdivision schematic, simplistic, incomplete and even inaccurate. This criticism is justified. However, I believe it can be useful to account, at a preliminary stage, for the richness and complexity of a debate that is far from being settled. For each approach I choose a few exemplary figures: Mario Mieli for the first, Michel Foucault and Judith Butler for the second, Leo Bersani and Lee Edelman for the third. I will also take briefly into account the thought of other authors (the already mentioned Guy Hocquenghem and Teresa de Lauretis, and then Eve Kosofsky Sedgwick, Jack Halberstam, Paul Preciado, Lisa Duggan, Jasbir Puar, Joseph A. Massad and Ann Cvetkovich, to name a few) in order to show the inadequacy of the proposed division in three paradigms, and, at the same time, to highlight the possibility of tracing back to each of them further developments of queer theories. I will present this tripartite division in the third chapter of this book, after addressing some preliminary questions in the first two.

In order to argue that queer theories are critical theories, it is thus necessary, before answering the question 'what are queer theories?', to answer the question 'what is critical theory?'. The latter question, in turn, generates other questions: 'what is political philosophy?', 'what is philosophy?', 'what is politics?'. And again, if politics can be defined as the field of human action characterised by the presence of power, a hypothesis that I borrow from the president of the Italian Society of Political Philosophy, Stefano Petrucciani (and soon it will be clear why I will refer to him) – then a further question we need to ask is 'what is power?'. The first chapter offers some possible answers to these questions. The second chapter deals instead with another problematic set of questions: if queer theories are political philosophies that critically examine, in different ways, the relationship (or juxtaposition) of politics to sexuality (and therefore of power to sexuality), then, 'what is sexuality?' Or rather, 'through which categories can we conceptualise sexuality?' 'What criteria define sexuality in current times?'. For those familiar with Foucault's thought, it won't be difficult to recognise its influence already in the way in which these questions are formulated. Moreover, as I have already mentioned, the French philosopher's analytics of power and of the specific dispositive of power which is sexuality – which he developed in *La volonté de savoir* (1976) – has represented a point of no return in the subsequent reflections on politics and sexuality, and a point of reference for the elaboration of queer theories since the 1990s.

It is precisely by virtue of Foucault's 'turning point' in political philosophy that in the third chapter I present, improperly, not only Foucault's thought, but also Freudo-Marxism, which such thought distances itself from, as queer theories – that is as 'queer theories' in quotation marks, insofar as they precede the theories that explicitly mark themselves as queer. Mine is, it goes without saying, an interpretation that can be challenged, like all the others that I will present in this book. This work, in fact, is not intended at all to settle the debate on the status and history of queer theories. Its ambition, on the contrary, is to keep such debate open, and to offer provisional conclusions in order to re-launch a future debate. Isn't this, after all, one of the tasks of any theoretical elaboration that aspires to secure a place in the realm of critical tradition? And isn't this what a good philosophy professor has to do in their classroom?

2. *Academic politics*. Indeed, I just said one of the tasks – not the only one. If I felt the need to write this book, it wasn't only for pedagogical and research reasons or for what I hope is the added heuristic value that a reflection on queer theories representative of my geographical positioning can contribute. There are also other positionings that structure this book, which are not only spatial, but also political. Whereas the situation of queer scholars in Italy is interesting as far as the elaboration of theoretical perspectives goes, when it comes to the academic world, and even more so when it comes to the public debate, being a queer scholar is a vulnerable condition that requires a certain amount of responsibility.

Because they occupy a liminal position between research-based and activist knowledge, and because of their critical, destabilising and disturbing character, queer theories cannot have a peaceful relationship with institutions in general, nor with academic institutions in particular. For queer theories, securing a space inside the university is definitely not a given, and if they want to secure it, they must know how to occupy it. And this is more difficult in some countries than in others. In Italy, in recent decades, an increasing number of established and precarious academic lecturers have been finding ways to teach feminist and queer theories, and an increasing number of students have been asking to write honours and doctoral theses on these topics. However, those who do research in these areas are at a disadvantage compared to those who do research in more traditional disciplines. In the absence of an official recognition, and in view of the increasing precarisation of academic work, those of us doing research on politics and sexuality have to legitimise their research time and again in front of their academic peers, and don't always find supportive panel members during job interviews and national evaluation procedures. Claims of this research's minor disciplinary relevance or pertinence constitute easy excuses to deny deserving scholars access to university positions. Those who, like me, have a secure position in academia have therefore the opportunity, if so inclined, to use their privilege to consolidate these studies' institutional position.

It is with these considerations in mind, that I supported the creation of the Research Centre PoliTeSse – Politics and Theories of Sexuality, which I currently direct, at the University of Verona in April 2012. In June 2018 PoliTeSse also organised at the University of Verona a conference entitled 'Studiare il genere e la sessualità nell'Università italiana' ['Researching gender and sexuality in the Italian university'], by inviting all the academic research groups that work on these issues in Italy. The conference was well and enthusiastically attended, and led to the establishment, in March 2019, of the GIFTS – the Gender, Intersex, Feminist, Trans-feminist and Sexuality studies – network, which promotes collaboration between established and precarious researchers, individuals or people affiliated with formal and informal research centres, associations, collectives, workshops, self-training groups and much more.

It is with all of this in mind, finally, that I wrote this book. Among other things, the book represents an attempt to open a debate among the Italian community of lecturers in Political Philosophy (that's why the reference to Petrucciani!) that would confirm the importance of the critical tradition in Political Philosophy, and especially of feminist and queer theories within it. One of the aims of the GIFTS network, in other words, is to affirm, among those who sit on political philosophy job interview committees and evaluation panels, the academic dignity of these discomfiting studies, whose disciplinary status remains uncertain. Precisely because of the discomfort they cause and their transdisciplinarity, these studies deserve to find a place – an interstitial, liminal place such as the one occupied by GIFTS and PoliTeSse, but nonetheless a place – in Italian academia.

3. Rights. What makes the position of queer scholars in Italy fragile, however, is not exclusively academic precarity and the opposition exercised by the academic professoriate. Those who do research and teach on the politics of sexuality also face attacks coming from outside the university, which sometimes stir outrage and solidarity in colleagues, and other times trigger dismissive reactions that can turn into mobbing.

In recent years in Italy, undeniable progress has been made, primarily in the legal sphere, with regard to the status of sexual minorities. When I wrote this book, the first Italian law that recognised same-sex couples had just been approved, even if just in the form of civil unions and not marriage – according to the law, civil unions do not constitute a family but a 'specific social formation' (Bill 20 May 2016, n. 76). Transgender people had also just been granted the right to change their gender without having to resort to the so-called 'surgical reassignment of sex' (Court of Appeal ruling of 20 July 2015, n. 15138; Constitutional Court ruling of 5 November 2015, n. 221). To this list, we should add other important international achievements regarding the depsychiatrisation of transgender people, some of which came after the publication of this book, and which also had repercussions in Italy. In 2013, in the fifth edition of the DSM (the *Diagnostical and Statistical Manual of Mental Disorders*, issued by the American Psychiatric Association), the transgender condition was downgraded from 'gender identity disorder' (an identity disorder, therefore a serious psychiatric disorder) to 'gender dysphoria' (a less severe mood alteration). In 2018, in the eleventh revision of the ICD (the *International Classification of Diseases* of the World Health Organization), 'gender incongruence' was moved from the chapter on mental disorders to a new chapter called 'Conditions related to sexual health', while the category 'transvestism' (which allowed psychologists and psychiatrists to accuse a transgender person of being affected by a paraphilia, dismissing thus the truth of their being) was completely deleted.

Despite all this, we must note that the 'Consensus Statement on Management of Intersex Disorders', which was signed in 2006 by the world's two most influential associations of paediatric endocrinology, the Lawson Wilkins Pediatric Endocrine Society and the European Society for Paediatric Endocrinology, is still largely disregarded in Italy. Our hospitals continue to perform genital mutilation on intersex infants, and for this reason, in 2016 – the same year as the approval of the law on civil unions – Italy was admonished by the Committee on the Rights of Persons with Disabilities of the United Nations for the violation of the integrity of the person.

This book obviously supports the achievements obtained by LGBTQI+ movements, is in favour of their full realisation, and encourages the attainment of rights that are still lacking in Italy (including the suspension of genital mutilation of intersex children; an anti-discrimination law explicitly naming hate crimes against sexual minorities; a more streamlined procedure for gender change; marriage and adoption for same-sex couples ...). Its political analysis, however, does not stop at the legal level. As will become clear, the book cautions against the risk that these same results may inscribe new vectors of power, that is, may impose new normative criteria on the lives of queer subjects. Moreover, this book gives an account of how, throughout the world, and particularly within Italian society, any progress in the achievement of rights for sexual minorities has been met with a strong reaction, which also directly invests the university and whoever works on gender studies and queer theories within it.

4. Verona. My experience at the University of Verona is, in this sense, paradigmatic. Back in 2010, during one of my courses on queer theories, a local newspaper, *L'Arena*, published letters of mothers worried about the content of my teaching, and the Catholic conservative association, Christus Rex, circulated a public note in which I was accused of teaching 'frocismo militante' [fag activism] – which is indeed another possible definition, and a very suitable one, of what I mean by 'queer theories'! Six years later, some members of 'Lotta studentesca' [Student Struggle], a youth organization linked to the neo-fascist party 'Forza Nuova', intervened in a confrontational way in one of my lectures – the course was dedicated that year to the history of the concept of gender – while others distributed leaflets that read: '"Lotta Studentesca Verona" will be present wherever there is a need to put our youth and the institutions that promote culture back on the right track'.

These actions were followed by others, which raised the stakes substantially. In May 2018 'Forza Nuova' announced that it was ready to prevent 'also by force' the holding of the conference titled 'Richiedenti asilo: Orientamento sessuale e identità di genere' [Asylum seekers: sexual orientation and gender identity], which PoliTeSse had organised together with the Hannah Arendt Centre for Political Studies, the departments of Human Sciences and Legal Sciences of the University of Verona, and three associations supporting migrant and

LGBTQI+ people, ASGI – Association for Legal Studies on Immigration, Association PINK and Arcigay Pianeta Milk-LGBT* Center. The rector of the University of Verona, Nicola Sartor, reacted by suspending the conference and releasing an equivocal note to the press, in which instead of simply condemning the neo-fascist group's threats, he covertly scolded those who had organised the initiative, placing Forza Nuova on the same level as the advocacy groups involved. The note stated that the event, dedicated to 'politically and ethically controversial issues', had 'abandoned the scientific sphere to become a terrain of confrontation and, above all, of search for visibility for different activists from a range of positions'. The rector's decision was quickly followed by a broad-based local, national and international mobilisation. A vigil was organised in Verona outside the Administration building to protest against the cancelling of the conference. Many associations and university research centres from all over Italy released public statements. An open letter was published in the French newspaper *Liberation* and in the Italian newspaper *Il manifesto*, which had very quickly gathered the signatures of more than 150 academics of international fame – among them, Etienne Balibar, Judith Butler, Lee Edelman, Christine Delphy, Éric Fassin, David M. Halperin, Paul B. Preciado, Chiara Saraceno and Joan W. Scott. The rector, now obviously fearful of losing face, quickly announced that an initiative centred on the same issues would be planned for September. The associations instead organised the same conference, though smaller, without university funds and outside of it altogether, on the day initially established, 25 May.

As the director of PoliTeSse, I immediately expressed my objection to the event being cancelled, and I later championed the rescheduling of the conference at the university, insisting on the involvement of all the associations initially present (involvement which was far from a given in the rector's intentions). Individually, however, I also participated in the protests and in the organisation of the May conference, giving a presentation there, and explicitly choosing not to be actively involved in the September event after the rector, in an interview with *L'Arena*, had defined as 'naïve' ASGI's, Pink's and Milk's choice not to wait for the new university conference. Indeed, it had not been a question of naivety, but of choice: the choice, shared by organisers and speakers, not to cower in front of the resurgence of fascism in Italy, and to manifest 'concern and dismay' (these were the feelings expressed in many of the public statements circulating at the time) at the lack of democratic backbone at the University of Verona. The university had indeed proved itself incapable, in the person of its rector, to grasp the incommensurable difference existing between seditious right-wing groups and advocacy activism for migrant and LGBTQI+ people (an advocacy specifically geared, it should be added, towards defending human rights established by international treaties ratified by Italy). Even though it was published before this regrettable episode, this book also seeks to delineate this incommensurable difference for the academic community and in public opinion – first of all in Verona but certainly not in Verona alone – by defending an idea of democracy driven by the agency of social movements.

5. *Italy*. In recent years, therefore, controversies surrounding the presence of PoliTeSse at the University of Verona have stepped far beyond the boundaries of the city, becoming a symptom of wider conflicts. In 2016, a new national newspaper called *La Verità* [The Truth] was founded, and soon it became the medium of expression of the right, even the extreme right, and of a new aggressive Catholicism allied to it. The University of Verona, its rector, and particularly PoliTeSse and its director, me, became prominent features in the newspaper from the onset, extensively used as examples of how a dangerous 'homosexualist' lobby has infiltrated academic institutions in order to disseminate a dangerous, and at the same time meaningless, education. With reference to this book, to give an example, on 12 July 2018 the journalist Patrizia Floder Reitter wrote an article entitled 'The queer delirium of the professor from Verona: Man or woman? It's just a convention'.

On 25 April 2017, however, the newspaper gave space to Lorenzo Fontana, at the time MEP of the Italian League party, who announced that his party would ask the government in Rome for clarification on the use of funds by the University of Verona, and stating that the university, instead of organising 'all these workshops on gender that concern a small minority of people', should have tackled issues related to 'employment, democracy, globalisation, businesses, the demographic decline, and the lack of families with children'. Fontana was interviewed by Floder Reitter herself, in a short article entitled 'The Euro MP wants to know who is paying'. In it Fontana stated that the most urgent issue of our current times is not 'that gay people may marry, that they may change sex, but the fact that we are dying out'. The question was tabled in the Italian parliament the following month by an MP of the same party, Massimiliano Fedriga, who pointed out that 'Lorenzo Bernini', in addition to being 'a researcher in political philosophy who writes about gender studies and queer theories (according to which there is no single way of being men and women, but a multiplicity of identities and experiences)', is also 'a fixed presence at many gay prides'.

Rector Sartor, already mortified by the numerous attacks against him in *La Verità*, where his photo had often been placed next to those of drag queens or half-naked muscle men, was compelled to write then a statement for the parliament to defend the teaching and research activity of PoliTeSse. And he probably did so reluctantly. This could explain, though not justify, the angry exasperation that led him in May 2018, to take such an ill-advised decision to suspend the conference on asylum seekers. The point here, however, is another one entirely. In the meantime, both Fontana and Fedriga's political careers have soared. Fedriga became the president of the Friuli Venezia Giulia region precisely in May 2018, whereas the following month Fontana – who in July 2017 had already been appointed as Deputy Mayor of Verona – became the Italian Minister for Family and Disabilities. When I first wrote this book, Italy was ruled by a centre-left coalition, the same coalition that led to the approval of the law on civil unions. However, at the time of this introduction, the government is instead formed by a coalition between the 5 Stars Movement and the League. The former portrays itself as an anti-system political force, neither right nor left. The latter is a right-wing party with strong ties to the extreme right, even to neo-fascist parties such as Forza Nuova and CasaPound Italia. And between the two political forces, it is undoubtedly the League that counts the most.

Both Fontana and Fedriga have excellent relations with the Federal Secretary of the League, Minister of the Interior and Vice-Prime Minister, and government's strong man, Matteo Salvini. And along with Salvini and the Minister of Education, University and Research, Marco Bussetti (gravitating as well around the League despite being an independent), they both intervened at the 13th World Congress of Families, held from 29 to 31 March 2019 in

Verona. The World Congress is an event organised each year in a different country in order to promote an international alliance between Christian groups (Catholics, different types of Protestants, Orthodox) officially to defend 'life' and the 'natural family', but in truth to oppose abortion and divorce rights, same-sex marriage and union rights, the implementation of inclusive education in schools and of gender and sexuality studies in universities. In addition to hosting the event in the prestigious 'Palazzo della Gran Guardia', the municipality of Verona (whose mayor is right-wing Federico Sboarina) appeared among the organisers of its thirteenth edition, which was sponsored by the Ministry for Family and Disabilities, the Friuli Venezia Giulia region, the Veneto region and the province of Verona.

A 'March for the Family' became the highlight of the event, in which a clearly visible group of Forza Nuova supporters paraded behind the fascist slogan 'God, Homeland, Family'. However, Verona also provided the stage for a full range of initiatives against this congress, which were organised by the local section, called Non Una di Meno, of the transnational feminist movement Ni Una Menos,[1] under the slogan 'Verona transfeminist city', and which ended with a huge march. This time, also the Italian academic community reacted promptly. PoliTeSse collaborated with Non Una di Meno in organising conferences and debates. The whole Department of Human Sciences at the University of Verona collected signatures to denounce the antiscientific character of the positions expressed by the associations organising the World Congress of Families. These included: the requirement of having parents of different gender for a child's harmonious psychophysical development; the idea that it is possible to 'heal' homosexuality; the thesis according to which abortion and divorce are the main causes of the demographic decline, and so forth. Similar condemnatory statements were released by other universities. GIFTS instead used different arguments, drafting a statement of protest against the presence at the Congress of the Minister of Education, University and Research, Marco Bussetti. The statement also claimed the scientific non-neutrality of gender and sexuality studies, stating that these studies 'recognise the value of self-determination, promote the establishment, defence and expansion of spaces of freedom for all marginalised subjects, and oppose all forms of oppression and discrimination'. Even the rector Sartor, this time, wanted to let the press know that he had refused the organisers' request to turn the University of Verona into the venue for the World Congress of Families. He did, however, forget to mention the fact that for months Non Una di Meno had tried to obtain permission for classroom use at the University of Verona for the initiatives of 'Verona transfeminist city', to no avail.

Professors accused of 'fag activism' and of 'queer delirium', and then neo-fascist groups using intimidating tactics outside the classrooms, threats, censorship, petitions, parades and counter-marches: this, in short, is the state of gender studies and queer theories in the Italian university, where this book took its cues from. This is the situation in which it tried to intervene.

6. *The world here and now.* A deep historical analysis would be necessary to understand what's happening in Italy. Such analysis should take into account: the presence of the Vatican on the national territory and its political influence; Italy's fascist past; that civil war which was the war of liberation from Nazi-fascism; the Lateran Treaty between Mussolini and the Catholic Church, which was renegotiated but never rejected by republican Italy …. However, such an analysis would not be sufficient if it did not also consider more recent processes of global and epochal import. Since the fall of the Berlin Wall in 1989, both in Europe and elsewhere, the great parties of the institutional left have progressively transformed from anti-capitalist into liberal forces, interested in safeguarding the global economic order. This has meant that the liberal left has accepted the demands of LGBTQI+ movements, to which the old communist left certainly wasn't open, but has also made the left unable to tackle the increase in social inequalities caused by the long economic crisis started in 2008, paving the way for an increase in support for right-wing parties, which we have been witnessing in Italy, Hungary, Poland, the United States and Brazil, in recent years. The increase in migratory phenomena since the 1990s and the new terrorist attacks and wars started after 11 September 2001, have contributed to the other half of the picture.

It has now become commonplace to speak of a new populist moment in international politics, but the expression is insufficient. If populism is defined by the opposition of people to an elite, the populism that is so successful today is characterised by the spread of right-wing ideologies that define both people and the elite through nationalist discourses, in which often the defence of 'life' and the 'natural family' is associated with xenophobia, supremacist ideologies and various types of racism. By supporting the World Congress of Families alongside the neo-fascist party Forza Nuova, and at the same time by closing its ports to ships rescuing migrants in the Mediterranean sea, Salvini's League party, for example, tells us *exactly which* life must be safeguarded, reproduced and defended (supposedly also from the alleged 'extinction' mentioned by Fontana, or from the pride parades that so shock Fedriga), and which life instead can be sacrificed. Salvini's campaign slogan was 'Italians first', but the Italian people addressed by the League are not formed by the totality of those who live in Italy, nor by those who are less well-off. This is not a class as in the Marxist tradition, but neither it is the outcome of a rational pact between individuals as in the contractual tradition. The Italian people referred to are instead a group of heteropatriarchal families of pure Italian blood and Catholic faith that is rhetorically invoked against a left-wing pro-Europe elite, which has allegedly taken vital resources away from this people, not only to serve the interests of bankers and financial speculators, but also to protect the rights of women and sexual minorities, as well as to welcome migrants and alleged Islamic terrorists on its shores. It's obvious that this is a 'people' that militants from Forza Nuova and other extreme right parties and movements have no difficulty identifying with.

Salvini calls himself a 'sovereignist' in opposition to neoliberal globalisation, but his populist demagogy is part of a moment in international politics, which, in Italy as elsewhere, is taking illiberal, undemocratic and even neo-fascist turns. Although it was written before the establishment of the 5 Stars/League government, this book, and its English translation, also intend to offer arguments to respond to these turns.

7. *Democracy*. The reorganisation of the Christian conservative front participating in this dark moment of global politics dates back to the mid-1990s, when the World Congress of Families was also founded. This coincided with a period in which the issue of LGBTQI+ rights was on the international

political agenda, and gender studies and queer theories were spreading to universities around the world. Since then, as a reaction, a transnational campaign was launched against these rights and studies, which produced that caricatural assemblage of rhetorical tropes called 'gender ideology'. In Italy, this campaign has been very successful. This can be confirmed by the fact that Fontana was appointed to the Ministry for Family and Disability, and that the World Congress of Families took place in Verona, in the palace of the Gran Guardia, which on 21 September 2013 had hosted the first major Italian public conference against this alleged ideology, which would then be re-proposed in many other places in the country.

Significantly, the title of that conference, 'The theory of gender: for or against Man?', was in the form of a question, which ideally occupies an important position among those questions that this book will attempt to answer. As a 'fag activist', I fully identify myself with the statement released by the GIFTS network at the World Congress of Families. The subject I research and teach, which is not called 'gender ideology' but 'queer theories', is, by no means, neutral. And yes, queer theories are indeed against Man: that is, against the hegemony of the white, endosex, cisgender, heterosexual man, a hegemony that an undemocratic and illiberal right is trying to reaffirm. This does not mean that queer theories are ideological, prescriptive or normative. As critical political philosophies, they take the side of democracy, understood not as a representative regime in which the will of the majority rules, but as a process in which, unlike what is happening in current populist and sovereignist rhetoric, the people are always to-come, they come into being through the exercise of citizenship by those who do not have citizenship.[2] If I have written this book, starting from my positioning within the university and within Italian society, and if two years after its publication I propose it in English translation, it is also, and especially, to defend this idea of radical democracy, which is also, and above all, an anti-fascist idea.

*

On 30 March, 2019, Salvini, before his speech at the World Congress of Families, published a post on Facebook that ended with a sarcastic reference to the demonstration of Non Una di Meno: 'I suggest that certain feminists who attack the family, should instead worry about the Islamic extremism that likes to submit, humiliate and maybe even beat women'. About ten days later, on a live video on Facebook, he commented on the upcoming 74th anniversary of the Liberation of Italy from Nazi-fascism with these words: 'On April 25, there will be parades of partisans and of those against partisans, of fascists and communists, of reds and blacks, of greens, blues, yellows and reds … We are in 2019 and I am not interested in the fascist-communist derby. I am interested in the future of our country'.

Actually, on 25 April 1945, no soccer match took place in Italy between fascists and communists, as if they were just two factions belonging to the same totalitarian systems of the last century. Instead, a war of liberation, which was also a civil war, ended. It was a war between fascists on the one hand and anti-fascists on the other, between totalitarianism and democracy. And this is still the case for those who celebrate that anniversary, even after the historical process that has led the greater part of the left from communism to neoliberalism, and that has allowed fascism, although in a 'new' version, to re-enter the scene by joining forces with right-wing Christians in the fight against immigration, against Islam, against the achievements by feminist and LGBTQI+ movements. No hypothetical future can erase a past that is still present.

The football metaphor used by Salvini was really distasteful, but allow me to use it again, at the end of this introduction, to reply to the vice-prime minister, and also to the rector of the University of Verona. If we were indeed to have a derby, then I have no doubt which of the two teams I play and intend to continue to play on, also with this book.

Verona, 25 April 2019

Notes

1 Translators' note: Non Una di Meno [No one woman less] is the Italian version of a transnational feminist movement to end violence against women that started as Ni Una Menos in Argentina in 2016. The Italian movement also started in 2016. More information can be found at https://nonunadimeno.wordpress.com.
2 Translators' note: Bernini's reference here is to Jacques Rancière's conception of democracy as an ongoing political exercise of power by those who are excluded from it in *Hatred of Democracy* (2006).

References

Foucault, M. (1976) *La volonté de savoir*. Paris: Gallimard.
Rancière, J. (2006) *Hatred of Democracy*. Translated by S. Corcoran. New York and London: Verso.

1 Critical theory and political philosophy

1.1 What is political philosophy?

Queer, as I will argue in the next pages, is a polysemic term, or better, a floating signifier, which transfers its own instability to the nouns it modifies when it is used as an adjective. This is especially true when queer accompanies the noun 'theory', which I would rather use in the plural: queer theories encompass a broad range of studies in which many different methodologies and opinions are at stake. Whether they apply to literature, cinema, art or society, or whether they are situated within the disciplines of anthropology, sociology or history, queer studies share a similar critical stance and are anchored to a few fundamental political principles, which will be examined later in this book. The purpose of this first chapter is to situate queer theories within the tradition of critical theory, which in turn can be situated within the larger tradition of political philosophy. Our first question will thus be: what do we mean by critical and political philosophy? Instead of finding an immediate answer, this question might generate more questions, in a kind of fractal progression: 'what is critical philosophy?', 'what is political philosophy?', and also 'what is philosophy', 'what is politics?'. This task already sounds exhausting. Moreover, it won't produce satisfying results, as it will be impossible to give *one* definitive answer to each of these questions. There may be more than one answer each time, and when one is selected it will be because of a specific choice of method or field, so as to enable me to trace a coherent trajectory towards a possible definition of queer theories.

While in Italy gender studies and queer theories do not have a specific institutional status, 'Political Philosophy' is the name of a discipline recognised by the Ministry of Education, University and Research. It is also the title of a university course within the Political and Social Sciences degree, listed as SPS/01. In the list of academic disciplines, there are other subjects considered similar to political philosophy: History of Political Theories (SPS/02), History of Political Institutions (SPS/03) and Political Science (SPS/04). These distinctions may sound spurious, and aimed mostly at differentiating academic posts, and I recognise they partially are. However, there is a deeper reason that distinguishes political philosophy from other similar disciplines: political philosophy examines political phenomena with the instruments of philosophy. We can consider valid what Leo Strauss stated in a renowned conference in 1955: 'Since political philosophy is a branch of philosophy, even the most provisional explanation of what political philosophy is cannot dispense with an explanation, however provisional, of what philosophy is' (1989, p.4). If, to begin with, political philosophy is the academic discipline that observes political phenomena through the lenses of philosophy, then in order to understand what political philosophy refers to, we need to start asking ourselves what we mean by philosophy, and what we mean by politics. In order to avoid an endless accumulation of references, I will rely here on prominent ideas, as Aristotle invites us to do when reliable premises are missing in dialectical arguments (1997, p.10). However, I won't consider the prestige of such ideas as a guarantee of truth.

Scholars generally recognise Socrates as the initiator of the Western philosophical tradition. He was sentenced to death in 399 BC by his Athenian fellow citizens because of his philosophical activity. Philosophy was accused of challenging traditional ideas and faith in the gods, and of corrupting the young; in brief, it represented a danger to the established order. We could thus define philosophy starting from its *function*, taking on board what Socrates' accusers believed, and state, by borrowing the title of a film by Pedro Almodovar, that the purpose of philosophy is *bad education*, [1] that is, challenging accepted truths in the community one belongs to, being critical of its institutions and causing trouble and disruption. In Plato's narrative, Socrates himself, in his fruitless attempt to defend himself, can't come up with anything better than to compare himself to a 'gadfly!'.[2] We could therefore argue that philosophy itself was constitutively born as political and critical philosophy, that is, as a practice of thought meant to enact forms of disturbance towards the 'polis'. Alternatively, we could attempt to define philosophy starting not from the function that it first acquired through Socrates in Athens, but from Socrates' way of practising it, that is, from his habit of asking his fellow citizens, in an exhaustive manner, the question: 'what is it?' and in contesting their answers each time. In the *Republic*, a dialogue that seeks to define what justice is, Plato asks Socrates to narrate the reaction of sophist Thrasymachus to this way of practising philosophy, a reaction of someone who seems to have lost his temper:

> But when we paused after I said this, he could keep still no longer; he coiled himself up like a wild beast crouching, and came at us as if to tear us to pieces. Polemarchus and I were both panic-stricken. What is this stale old nonsense you are babbling, Socrates he roared out in the midst of the company. And why do you keep politely deferring to each other like simpleminded fools? If you truly wish to know what the just is, do not merely ask questions or refute out of emulousness when someone suggests an answer because you know it is easier to ask than to answer. Answer for yourself, and say what you claim the just to be. And see to it that you do not tell me it is the obligatory or the useful or the beneficial or the profitable or the advantageous, but state clearly and precisely what you mean, because I will not accept it if you talk stuff like that.
>
> (2005, p.13; 336 b-d)

Since its origins, therefore, philosophy has been compared by its opponents to a useless mental exercise, to a meaningless 'chat', that those who need certainties and easy answers find irritating. Its unproductive nature was even more stigmatised in the beginning, when philosophy was not yet divulged through written texts, but through discussions so polite as to be unnerving. Thrasymachus indeed reproaches Socrates and Polemarchus of 'politely deferring to each other like simpleminded fools'. However, back then as well as now, philosophy not only requires patience, good manners and steady nerves. It also, and especially, requires courage. Its radical questioning does not stop at anything or anyone: not at beliefs that seem obvious and natural; not at the teachings and precepts that come from the authorities; not at the opinions held within the intellectual circles to which the philosopher belongs; not even at the vehemence and violence of those who want to silence philosophy 'by tearing to pieces' those who practise it (Plato will follow Socrates' example after his death). It is no coincidence that Thrasymachus, who in this passage lashes out against a thought that proceeds by formulating problems and not by asserting dogmas, will affirm in the rest of the *Republic* that justice is the advantage of the stronger. Without delving into the details of Plato's definition of justice as the harmony of the parts, it is important to stress here that Socrates inaugurates philosophy by way of asking the wise men of Athens the 'what is' question, with the intention of refuting their answers. Following his example, I will attempt to apply this method to the subject I teach, examining some of the views of those who addressed the issue before me. Like Socrates, I will talk to my fellow citizens, and in particular to the academics, since I am an academic myself, with the ideal aim of opening up a debate on the philosophical-political status of feminism and queer theories.

My first wise man is Stefano Petrucciani, Professor of Political Philosophy at the University La Sapienza in Rome and currently second-term president of the Italian Society of Political Philosophy (SIFP). Among his many books we find also the textbook *Modelli di filosofia politica* [Models of Political Philosophy], which, similarly to what I do in this book, begins with the attempt to define political philosophy by resorting to some authoritative voices in the field. Just as I did, Petrucciani also follows Leo Strauss's suggestions and starts by going after the meaning of the term 'philosophy', reaching a definition that I believe owes to Jürgen Habermas's thought. Habermas delineates philosophy neither through the Socratic *practice* of questioning, nor through its political *function*, but through selecting Socrates's research *method* and the *object* such method is applied to as the criteria for its definition. Petrucciani states that philosophy is 'a refined and institutionalized form of discourse whose method consists in the use of *public, critical and open reasoning*' (2003, p.8).[3] If he is right, according to this method the Western philosophical tradition can be described as an uninterrupted and still ongoing discussion, which started with the questions that Socrates asked his fellow citizens. Everyone can potentially intervene in this discussion, provided that one complies with the specific parameter set out by Habermas (1998) in his theory of communicative action: the logic of the best argument. According to this logic, what counts in a philosophical discussion are the most persuasive arguments; not the strength, power or charisma of the person who speaks, but the most rational and convincing argument, the one that manages to refute the arguments of the opponents and challenge them to further refutations. Philosophers thus know very well that every outcome of their philosophical reasoning is provisional and open to the criticism of those who come after them. Their philosophical practice is non-dogmatic, anti-authoritarian and offers a contribution to the field of public discourse, which in fact is one of such practice's own condition of possibility (Habermas, 1989). For Petrucciani, however, the provisional status of philosophy's achievements depends only in part on philosophy's own research method. It is also the very object of research that turns philosophy into an endless practice.

According to Petrucciani,

> as to the object, [philosophy] confronts the issue of our own orientation in the world – an issue that is as inescapable as it is (perhaps) inexhaustible and one that cannot be addressed by the empirical sciences because they themselves need legitimation and orientation.
>
> (2003, pp.8–9)

Thus, if the method of philosophical questioning clearly separates philosophy from revealed religions, where truth is entrusted to sacred texts or communicated directly by the deity, its object of research differentiates it also from what Petrucciani calls the 'empirical sciences'. Philosophy's relationship with empirical data is, in fact, never direct. Indeed, even when philosophy invokes experience, such experience is not confined to the individual but is characterised by an intersubjective dimension, which requires the consensus of others in the public sphere (and this idea is present both in Habermas's theory of communicative action and in Kant's (1790/2007) theory of aesthetic judgement). For Petrucciani, this has to do with the fact that the questions formulated by philosophy, even when it analyses facts, are questions about orientation, direction and meaning. An example might help clarify this further. When Hannah Arendt examines the political reality of the twentieth century, the purpose of her research, which is nonetheless based on historical facts, is not to establish the truth of the facts but rather to interpret them in a meaningful dimension. When Arendt uses the concept of 'totalitarianism' (1951), she highlights the radical discontinuity that the fascist and communist regimes of the twentieth century mark with respect to previous political experiences, particularly past tyrannies and dictatorships. Faced with the extermination of millions of Jews by the Nazi regime, Arendt probes the nature of the evil that was at work in that historical event, coming to the well-known conclusion that this was a sort of 'banal' evil (1963), caused by habits of obedience and lack of critical thought. The value of Arendt's theses stems not only from their adherence to historical truth, but also from their effects of political truth. To put it in Petrucciani's terms, it stems from the way in which they orient Arendt's readers in the world they share with other human beings. In other words, the concept of the 'banality of evil' isn't circumscribed to the description of a given regime's functioning. It is a call not to forget the importance of political thought and political action,[4] and to resist any regime that tries to smother their unfolding.

This example allows us to take a further step. If philosophy is the discursive practice that applies the method of the best argument to the problem of the orientation of human beings in the world, then political philosophy will be that philosophy that will use the same method to ask questions of direction concerning politics, as Arendt does in her analysis of the totalitarianisms of her time. 'But then, what is politics?', Socrates would ask at this point. Petrucciani would reply that politics is that sphere of human experience characterised by the presence of 'power relations' and thus that power is the specific object to which political philosophy applies its method of the best argument. 'So then, I can hear Socrates asking again – what exactly is power?' As Petrucciani states:

> If asked about this point, political philosophers would give very different answers: the most canonical tradition of political philosophy examined institutionalized forms of power, represented

by laws and government institutions; whereas it was especially heterodox philosophers who insisted that the most fundamental power relations are found outside canonical government institutions and outside the law, in property relations (Marx) or in the 'micro-physics of power' (Foucault).[5] These heterodox thinkers will not be wronged, however, if we say that political philosophy has to do mainly with institutionalized forms of power, which, from a certain point in human history onward, can be defined as state power.

(2003, p.6)

Therefore, claiming that power is the main object of investigation of political philosophy does not settle the issue – on the contrary, it is a way to open it up further. Those who practise political philosophy are divided on the question of what constitutes power, and which power relations are philosophically relevant.

Like every definition of political philosophy, Petrucciani's is also the result of a firm and specific choice. In addition to Habermas, he refers to a well-established theoretical tradition in modernity, which he presents as 'canonical', and whose origins can be traced back to the seventeenth-century theory of contractualism, and specifically back to Thomas Hobbes. According to this tradition (which Arendt holds responsible for the processes of depoliticisation that led to totalitarianism), politics coincides with the administration of the State and the exercise of violence necessary to it. In addition, political power essentially coincides with the State's ability to make subject/citizens obey, ultimately through the sanctions the State can impose on those who transgress the law. In fact, Petrucciani defines political power, using Max Weber's famous words, as the 'monopoly of the legitimate use of physical force' (Weber, 1946, p.78). These words can be contrasted with those, equally famous, of Carl Schmitt, according to whom 'the concept of State presupposes the concept of the political' (1932/1996, p.19) and not vice versa.

To define politics through power, and power through the State, which is itself a political organisation, is clearly a vicious circle. The State is after all only one historical form of political power among others. For Schmitt the concept of politics, or more precisely the criterion for defining politics, is to be found in the distinction between friend and enemy. A political community is in place when someone (the sovereign) is able to delineate the boundaries between those who belong to the community and those who are excluded from it, and thus can be killed. This definition also, however, can be situated in the wake of the modern tradition initiated by Hobbes's theory of sovereignty, and it only goes halfway towards understanding how queer theories can count as political philosophies. Indeed, queer theories examine forms of power that are only partially, and not always, exercised 'from above' by the apparatuses of the State and by the law. On the contrary, their attention often turns to normative devices that operate across the whole fabric of society, nesting in the most intimate human relations and playing a role in shaping individual subjectivity. In order to understand the political status of queer theories, we need then to distance ourselves from a 'canonical' way of theorising politics, and approach those 'heterodox thinkers' whom Petrucciani declares to not want to dismiss, while all along doing exactly that. Karl Marx, as Petrucciani reminds us here, showed that, in the modern era, power acts not only through the apparatuses of the State but also, and above all, through the ownership of the means of production. The feminist tradition, which Petrucciani here seems to forget, has shown how the power of the modern State can preserve intact a much more archaic structure of power, patriarchy. In their understanding and problematising of not only the power of men over women, but also that of heterosexual cisgender men over heterosexual and lesbian women, gay men, transgender people, bisexual and intersex people and all sexual minorities, contemporary queer theories also owe a great deal in particular to the 'Copernican revolution' achieved by Foucault's analytics of power.

In an interview published in 1982, Foucault proposed a definition of power, which mirrors that of Weber. Such definition not only does not include the State, and thus avoids the vicious circle denounced by Schmitt, but is also based on the difference between power and violence. As Foucault argues, violence 'acts upon a body or upon things; it forces, it bends, it breaks on the wheel, it destroys, or it closes the door on all possibilities' (1982, p.789). Power, on the contrary, is 'an action upon an action, on existing actions or on those which may arise in the present or the future': it thus implies that 'the one over whom power is exercised be thoroughly recognized and maintained to the very end as a person who acts; and that … a whole field of responses, reactions, results and possible interventions may open up' (1982, p.789). In other words, violence reduces the subject to passivity, leaving them no possibility to act, whereas power relies on the subject's ability to act (it acts upon their actions), and on their freedom to resist. Power is thus exercised not only through the State apparatus but is present whenever a person is capable of influencing someone else's actions, and thus is found in all social and interpersonal relationships, even the most intimate ones. Moreover, this power is not limited to restrictions, prohibitions and interdictions; on the contrary power is *productive* not only of a range of possible actions, but also of the very subjects that are involved in enacting them. This is the second change of perspective that Foucault carries out in relation to those early modern notions of power to which Weber, Schmitt and even Petrucciani, although differently, owe their theorisations.

As I have anticipated, at the origin of this modern notion of power we can place Thomas Hobbes, who, in *Leviathan* (1651/2012) tries to justify the necessity of State sovereignty on the basis of the nature of human beings, as he argues that in the absence of the State individuals would wage war on each other. Only the threat of punishment, therefore, can maintain a condition of relative peace. According to Hobbes, people establish the State through a rational pact. In order to escape the miserable and dangerous conditions in which they would find themselves if they merely indulged in their passions, they appoint a ruler to represent them and whose will they recognise as their own. Foucault instead, in works like *Discipline and Punish* (1975/1995) and *The Will to Knowledge* (1976/1998), radically overturns this hypothesis, stating that most of the time it is not individuals that institute power, but it is power that shapes subjectivities. Still nowadays, Hobbes's theory of representative State sovereignty allows us to answer questions such as, 'under what conditions, and for what reasons, is a citizen obliged to obey the laws of the State to which we belong?' and 'what justifies the authority with which the sovereign body, for example the parliament, proclaims the law?'. Foucault instead allows us to ask a set of very different questions: 'what power mechanisms make citizens obey the laws of the State to which they belong?', 'how did they learn to recognise the will of the sovereign as legitimate?'.

Let's think of a university lecture, which involves primarily two types of actors: the professor (usually one) and the students (usually many). The professor requires the students to remain silent and still for the duration of the lecture. However, this is an exercise of power and not of violence, because students were not forcefully taken into the classroom and are not forced to remain silent and still because they are tied to chairs and gagged. Students have entered the classroom voluntarily, and voluntarily they remain silent and take notes, although they could do many other things in the classroom (like singing, for example, or loudly insulting the professor). If they remain silent and take notes, it is because they are involved in a power relationship capable of co-opting their will. Of such relationship the teacher is a vector, but also a product. There are a number of underlying conditions that make the professor's power 'work'. Among them are: the social capital guaranteed by a degree in the job market; the prestige conferred by culture; university regulations; and a complex education system that formed both their students and themselves. Hobbes himself, in *On the Citizen*, admits that considering human beings as individuals who are unrelated corresponds to the pretence of thinking about them 'as if they had just emerged from the earth like mushrooms and grown up without any obligation to each other' (1642/1998, p.102).[6] In reality, as experience teaches us even before feminism, every human being is born a vulnerable infant, given birth to by a woman,[7] and determinants of geography, culture, religion, class, sex, race and dis/ability influence the way in which that infant will become an adult. These elements constitute thus power constraints, which limit people's freedom and at the same time make it possible. Not everyone has the privilege of getting access to university, and those who have it arrive there through a long period of training. Children are not naturally able to sit silently for hours taking notes, and only an educational system that begins at the nursery level can succeed in producing them as docile university students. Similarly, their teacher underwent the same training, and in addition, had to learn other skills that enabled them to transmit knowledge by speaking for a sustained period of time. Similarly, the interpretive perspective introduced by Foucault enables us to read other processes of subject formation. Not only the identities of students and teachers, but also those of workers and industry managers; of rulers and ruled; of citizens and members of parliament; of women and men[8] (as well as lesbians, gays, transgender people); of black and white people; of able and disabled people, are the result of complex power mechanisms in which freedom is always present, but never absolutely so.

The theories of 'the most canonical tradition of political philosophy', as Petrucciani calls it, are simply not enough to account for these forms of power. It is for this reason that against categories such as sovereignty and representation, Marx juxtaposed the notions of capital and of relations of production (1867/1990, 1885/1992, 1894/1992); feminism juxtaposed the category of patriarchy, and Foucault underscored categories such as disciplinary power, bio-power, pastoral power and the dispositive of sexuality.[9] I won't expand here on each of these concepts,[10] but naming them allows me to add something to my attempt to define political philosophy. So far I have described political philosophy, following Petrucciani and thus Habermas and the modern tradition from which he draws, as an endless discussion around questions regarding power. However, other definitions of political philosophy are possible as well.

For example, in 1991 – while Habermas was about to become one of the most celebrated philosophers of the European Union[11] – Gilles Deleuze and Félix Guattari (1994) dedicated an impassioned and deliberately 'unrestrained' (2) volume to the question *What is Philosophy?*, which reads:

> Every philosopher runs away when he or she hears someone say, 'Let's discuss this'. Discussions are fine for roundtable talks, but philosophy throws its numbered dice on another table. The best one can say about discussions is that they take things no farther, since the participants never talk about the same thing. Of what concern is it to philosophy that someone has such a view, and thinks this or that, if the problems at stake are not stated? And when they are stated, it is no longer a matter of discussing but rather one of creating concepts for the undiscussable problem posed. Communication always comes too early or too late, and it comes to creating, conversation is always superfluous. Sometimes philosophy is turned into the idea of a perpetual discussion, as 'communicative rationality', or as 'universal democratic conversation'. Nothing is less exact, and when philosophers

criticize each other, it is on the basis of problems, and on a plane that is different from theirs and that melt down the old concepts in the way a cannon can be melted down to make new weapons. It never takes place on the same plane. To criticize is only to establish that a concept vanishes when it is thrust into a new milieu, losing some of its components, or acquiring others that transform it. But those who criticize without creating, those who are content to defend the vanished concept without being able to give it the forces it needs to return to life, are the plague of philosophy.

(p.28)

If we read these words carefully, we gather that Deleuze and Guattari are not stating that philosophy does not engage with the philosophical tradition and with the views of other philosophers, nor are they saying that critical theory does not have philosophical status. On the contrary, in proposing their definition of philosophy, they offer a critique of the notion of philosophy, which has become mainstream in Europe since the late 1980s – and whose echo also resonates in Petrucciani's handbook – by way of a theoretical discussion with Habermas. Deleuze and Guattari want to emphasise the creative character of philosophical critique, whose aim is not only to refute opinions and demolish certainties, but also to build visions of the world and create new realities. Their philosophy constitutes also an answer to those who keep defining philosophy as the search for truth.[12]

For Deleuze and Guattari, in fact, the philosopher is 'the friend of concepts', the one who 'imagines and invents them', while 'philosophy is the art of forming, of inventing, of creating concepts' (1994, p.2). And the concepts are neither true nor false: rather, they produce truth effects. What I said earlier about Arendt and the question of totalitarianism can therefore be reiterated in relation to Marx and the concept of capitalism, in relation to Foucault and the concept of biopolitics, or even – as we shall see – in relation to Teresa de Lauretis and queer theories or Judith Butler and the question of gender. We can therefore say that, if philosophy invents, or reinterprets, concepts, political philosophy invents or reinterprets political concepts, which can bring forth new problems and new realities in the field of power. As to what exactly power *is*, however, philosophers keep disagreeing. One way to better understand what political philosophies are is to try to classify them according to the problems they look at, the questions they ask, the methodologies they adopt. This is what I will try to do now, moving again – as Aristotle teaches us – from the opinions of scholars, in order to differentiate critical theories from other ways of practising political philosophy.

1.2 Philosophies of universal questions and ontologies of actuality

For a long time, the written word has been the primary means through which philosophy has been elaborated, preserved and transmitted; philosophy, however, continues to be practised and transmitted orally and preserved through memory. In addition to producing concepts, Deleuze and Guattari remind us that philosophy produces its friends, that is, the philosophers. These are subjects who talk, they aren't just subjects who write. Moreover, although we often tend to forget it, philosophers are embodied human beings, equipped with a body and a personal history, with emotions, passions and feelings as well as reason. The majority of them nowadays work in universities, where they give lectures and participate in conferences, where they establish relations of friendship not only with concepts but also with their colleagues, their research directors and their students. The academic writing style privileges, however, the genre of the treatise over that of biography, the impersonal form over the first-person 'I', cold reasoning over accounts of conversations from which the warmth of affects may transpire. Thus, despite knowing that I will be transgressing conventions, I will not be silent on the fact that the second thinker with whom I will now open a dialogue was my mentor at the University of Milan, where he teaches History of Political Philosophy, despite technically belonging to a slightly different sector of the discipline (History of Political Doctrines, whose code is SPS/02). I want to reveal that not only I admire him, but I also consider him a dear friend and have feelings of gratitude and affection towards him. It was Marco Geuna who taught me to begin every academic course with the question 'what is political philosophy?' and to suggest that I include in my teaching programme Petrucciani's textbook *Models of Political Philosophy*. During his classes, which I had the privilege to attend at the University of Milan, instead of following the philosophical approach by Habermas endorsed by Petrucciani, Geuna preferred to discuss philosophy by making a distinction between two methods or styles of theory.

He used to explain that 'there are philosophies that ask universal questions and philosophies that ask questions of the present'. I will now try to give an account of this distinction, adding some personal considerations to my recollection of his classes.

The author that Geuna would regularly use to illustrate the philosophies of universal questions is Kant, who, in the *Critique of Pure Reason*, identifies three fundamental questions, which he believes can encapsulate all philosophical issues. These are: 'what can I know?', 'what should I do?', 'what can be hoped for?'. In his *Lectures on Logic*, Kant adds to these a fourth question that should include all the others: 'what is the human being?'. Philosophy for Kant qualifies thus as an anthropology – more precisely as an investigation of the limits of human rationality when it makes claims to universality. For Kant philosophy aims to solve recurrent problems, which allegedly regard humanity as a whole, always and everywhere. Kant answers the first question, 'what can I know?', by declaring his trust in science, which, however, he restricts to well-defined boundaries. According to him, human beings can know with certainty what they experience through the senses, and can discover the laws of Newtonian physics; they cannot, however, answer in a scientific manner questions of orientation such as: 'what is history for?', 'what is the best political constitution?', 'what is the meaning of human existence?', 'is there life beyond death?', and paradoxically also 'what are the limits of human knowledge?'. For Kant these questions can't be properly answered by science, yet they are unavoidable for human beings. And if the last question corresponds to the first of philosophy's foundational questions, insofar as it defines the scope of gnoseology (philosophy of knowledge), the other questions concern the field of deontology (moral philosophy) and the philosophy of religion: 'what should I do?', 'what is it to be hoped for?'. Since these questions do not concern the knowledge of natural phenomena, which can be experienced through the senses, they require the use of a rationality other than the scientific one (which nonetheless retains a universal character for Kant). This is especially valid for political philosophy, which Kant considers to be part of moral philosophy. In the philosophical project *Toward Perpetual Peace* Kant argues, for example, that *each* nation should aspire to a republican constitution (in which legislative power is separated from executive power), and that *all* States should come together in a worldwide federation of republics. This institution would represent the *universal* aim of politics as it would be the only one capable of ensuring peace, and every citizen of every State in the world should strive to achieve this aim in the name of an imperative of reason.

Perpetual Peace represents thus a clear example of the political philosophy of universal questions. Kant in this essay raises questions concerning the purpose and management of political power from the point of view of all human beings, as if it were possible to think of them without spatio-temporal specificities, and especially as if the philosophers were able to avoid them altogether. Other philosophers instead examine politics moving from, and in relation to, their own present. This is the case for Hegel, who in the preface to *Elements of the Philosophy of Right*, as Geuna used to explain in his lectures in Milan, described philosophy as 'its own time comprehended in thoughts' (Hegel, 1820/2003, p.21) and as 'the owl of Minerva [that] begins its flight only with the onset of the dusk' (p.23). Just like everyone else, in fact, for Hegel the philosopher also is '*a child of his time*', and his research is linked to 'what is' (p.21), especially when it concerns juridical and political topics. According to this perspective, the task of political philosophy is not to design an ideal universal model of coexistence on the basis of which to shape reality, but to understand the logic sustaining current political conditions. This philosophy must therefore look towards the past and not towards the future, in order to understand the history that led to the present situation, like goddess Minerva's 'owl', symbol of wisdom, that takes flight at dusk when 'a shape of life has grown old' (p.23). Thus, if Kant, in an age of conflict and political upheaval such as the late eighteenth century, goes as far as to imagine the possibility of a world federation of States that would bring about peace, Hegel's political philosophy, as Marx states in his *Critique of Hegel's Philosophy of Right* (1843/1970) can be instead accused of simply providing a justification for the political situation of the early nineteenth century, wherein the world – or at least Europe – was divided in States at war with one another within an economic regime of capitalist competition. However, not every philosophy that investigates the present has an apologetic aim.

This is not the case, for example, with Foucault, who, in a famous lecture at the Collège de France in 1983, defines his way of practising philosophy through the paradoxical expression 'ontologie de l'actualité' (2008, p.22).[13] Whereas in the metaphysical tradition Being (òntos is its Greek genitive form) is what coincides with itself and never changes, Foucault proposes to investigate being as it unfolds in the present, by reconstructing its history[14] in view of its potential change in current times. Foucault's intent is thus to examine the present not to legitimate and preserve the institutions of his time but to criticise them – just as Socrates was accused of doing with the Athenian institutions. This requires, first of all, a self-distancing move wherein one assumes a critical stance towards what seems self-evident about the subject of research his/her/them self. In fact, the ontology of actuality, for Foucault, is also and first of all an 'ontology of ourselves' (2010, p.21).

I will later show the importance of this thesis for queer theories, which (among other things) offer a critical examination of the history of the signifiers through which we currently classify sexual identities according to strict binaries (woman-man, transgender-cisgender, homosexual-heterosexual). For the moment I want to stress that, while Geuna, in his classification of philosophies, juxtaposes Hegel and Kant, in this lecture Foucault instead considers both Hegel and Kant as precursors of his philosophical practice. Specifically, Foucault makes a clear distinction in Kant's work, between the studies characterised by a universalist approach, such as those contained in the *Critique of Pure Reason* (1781/2008) and in the *Lectures on Logic* (1800/1992) – and which Geuna draws upon – and Kant's critical studies of the present, even ascribing to two of his minor works, 'An Answer to the Question: What is Enlightenment?' (1784/2006b) and 'The Contest of the Faculties' (1758/2006c), the inception of the modern tradition of the ontology of actuality. In these essays, Kant takes a position within the debates of his own time, questioning the meaning of the philosophy of Enlightenment, and therefore of his own philosophy, in relation to the French Revolution – that is, questioning the role of the philosopher, of himself as a philosopher, in his current political times. This provides us with a further definition of political philosophy, according to which philosophy becomes properly political when it includes the philosopher's participation in the public debates of his[15] time, thus becoming a political act on the plane of thought. In *What is Philosophy?* Deleuze and Guattari insist precisely on the fact that Foucault's intentions orient his philosophical practice towards the 'actual' and not on the present.

> The actual is not what we are but, rather, what we become, what we are in the process of becoming-that is to say, the Other, our becoming-other. The present, on the contrary, is what we are and, thereby, what already we are ceasing to be. We must distinguish not only the share that belongs to the past and the one that belongs to the present but, more profoundly, the share that belongs to the present and that belonging to the actual. It is not that the actual is the utopian prefiguration of a future that is still part of our history. Rather, it is the now of our becoming. When Foucault admires Kant for posing the problem of philosophy in relation not to the eternal but to the Now, he means that the object of philosophy is not to contemplate the eternal or to reflect history but to diagnose our actual becomings: a becoming-revolutionary that, according to Kant himself, is not the same thing as the past, present, or future of revolutions.
>
> (1994, pp.112–113)

Political philosophy understood as ontology of actuality is therefore not contemplation of an eternal being, but participation in the becoming of being. Although such philosophy 'begins its flight only at dusk', as it investigates history in order to understand the present, its temporality is neither past, present nor future. When understood as an ontology of the actual, political philosophy becomes a form of thought that changes the subjects who practice it here and now, that is, in actuality.

This philosophy asks questions such as: 'what have we become by virtue of our history?', 'what can we do now with ourselves?' and 'how can our thought contribute to this change?'. Moreover, if it is true that the philosopher is 'the child of his time', as Hegel (1820/2003) states, even political philosophies that claim to investigate the universal can only investigate *the political universal of their own historical time* (a paradoxical expression, as much as Foucault's 'ontologie de l'actualité'), that is, they can only think through what can be a universal political solution for their own time, and support ways to achieve it. When Hobbes, moving from the fiction of the state of nature, proposes the sovereign-representative State as the universal form of politics, he is also intervening in the English public debates of his time. He proposes the autonomy and unity of the State both as an antidote to the imperial and papal powers, and to the division of Christians between Catholics and Protestants (which were causing violent conflicts), and as a solution to the Thirty Years War (1618–1642) and the British Civil War (1642–1648). The seventeenth century was in fact the century in which European States consolidated their power following the breakdown of the unity of Christianity. Hobbes participates in these historical events by offering new concepts for theorising politics: however, the universal concept he proposes – i.e. the State – is a *historical* universal. We can say the same of Kant's political proposal. It is symptomatic that *Toward Perpetual Peace* was composed on the occasion of the Peace of Basel of 1795, signed by revolutionary France and by Prussia. The project of a world federation of republics at the time of Kant is certainly visionary but is also strongly grounded in historical reality. It reflects the aspirations of the Prussian citizen in Kant – someone who lived in a Europe where the French Revolution had given powerful resonance to Republican ideals that made more obvious than ever the injustices committed by colonial powers.

Therefore, every authentically *political* philosophy – even when it presents itself as the search for the universal in line with the platonic aspiration for the philosopher's exit from the 'cave' of the human condition (Plato, 2005, pp.514b–520a) – participates in current reality, insofar as it constitutes an intervention in the public debates of the philosopher's own time. In some cases, as with Hobbes and Hegel, it interprets and acquiesces in historical processes as they unfold; in others, as in the case of Kant, it seeks solutions to solve the problems of the present. In some other cases, as with those 'gadflies' (Plato, 2005) of politics such as Socrates and Foucault, it performs a condemning and disturbing function, and imparts a 'bad education'[16] aimed at undermining the current situation without apparently offering alternatives. To better understand these different philosophical approaches, the distinction between philosophies of universal questions and ontologies of actuality is not sufficient. Instead, we need to introduce another set of distinctions within political philosophy: that between realistic, normative and critical philosophies.

1.3 Political, realistic, normative and critical philosophies

In the above-mentioned *Modelli di filosofia politica*, Petrucciani, recalling the father of Italian political studies, Norberto Bobbio (1999), identifies two fundamental approaches of political philosophy: the realistic and the normative one. The first belongs to those philosophies that investigate 'the nature of political action and its definition' (Petrucciani, 2003, p.11) and asks structural questions about the functioning of power and politics as they manifest in reality. In other words, this approach investigates the essence of politics, and its fundamental questions are: 'what is politics?', 'what is power?' and 'what does it mean to act politically?'. The normative approach characterises those philosophies that try to solve 'the question of what constitutes the best political system' and 'the question of what is political obligation based on (that is, why, and especially whom we must obey)' (2003, p.11). This approach does not therefore investigate politics as it is, but politics as it should be. Normative philosophies cannot avoid engaging with a preliminary analysis of reality, choosing from it some significant elements such as, for example, people's needs and passions, their way of thinking, or their moral purposes, which might serve as premises for their prescriptive arguments. Realistic philosophies have a normative aspect too, since their purpose is to prescribe which model of action is appropriate to the nature of politics. The two approaches are therefore interrelated, but they produce different theoretical styles according to which of the two prevails.

Realistic philosophies are generally understood as philosophies, which do not limit themselves to stating, like Machiavelli does, that they want to investigate the 'effectual truth' of politics. Rather, they come to a similar conclusion as Machiavelli, that this reality coincides with the struggle for power, and that the task of those who engage in politics is to participate in this struggle, setting aside moral concerns that would lead them to their 'ruin' rather than to their 'preservation'.[17] It would be simplistic, however, to argue that political realists presume a separation between politics and morals, while normative philosophies subordinate the former to the latter. It is true that among political realist philosophers, there are those who argue, like the aforementioned Thrasymachus in Plato's *Republic*, that in politics justice is nothing but the advantage of the stronger, that is, what is imposed by law by the one who wins in the struggle for power. Among the political realists, however, there are also those who argue, like Weber (1946), that although the good politician cannot avoid participating in the struggle for power, *he* (for Weber the politician is always male) must nonetheless be driven by good intentions. We should remember that for Weber the State coincides with the monopoly of the legitimate use of physical force, and in their quest for legitimisation, politicians must also deal with the dimension of values. In any case, followers of the realistic approach, including Weber, believe that politics has an inevitable conflictual and warlike dimension, and that the use of force and violence are intrinsic aspects of the struggle for power. Schmitt (1932/1996), as I previously mentioned, goes as far as defining the political community through the distinction between friend and enemy, wherein the enemy is understood as the one who can be physically eliminated. Realistic political philosophies are also often characterised by a strong anthropological pessimism. Schmitt believes, for example, that only theories that move from the idea of human 'wickedness' are truly political. He therefore turns Hobbes into the paradigm of political philosophy, for his lucid affirmation that 'man is a wolf to man'[18] (1642/1998, p.3), and that only well-armed rulers are able to restrain their citizens' violent passions and defend them from other rulers.

Anthropological pessimism, however, isn't a trait of political realism only. Even the pacifist Kant believes that 'nothing entirely straight can be fashioned from the crooked wood of which humankind is made' (1784/2006d, p.9). Kant, however, elaborates a normative political philosophy because from this assumption he concludes that it is precisely human imperfection that makes morality possible, insofar as this latter is conceived as the duty to avoid selfish instincts and fulfil the imperatives of reason. Normative political philosophies therefore are not, or at least not always, illusions for kind souls: they represent attempts to develop moral and/or rational criteria on the basis of which to formulate political judgements. Political normative philosophies provide a variety of answers to questions such as: 'which regimes deserve obedience, and which ones need instead to be modified or overturned?', 'what values must political action inspire, despite the fact that the world is imperfect?' and 'is the aim of the political community the achievement of justice and furthermore the common good; or is it the guarantee of freedom or, even further, of equality?'. For both Hobbes and Kant, for example, peace is one of the fundamental aims of politics; however, the former prefers the absolute State, better if monarchic, while the latter prefers a republican constitution, or rather a world federation of republics. In addition to their preferences regarding the best form of government, normative political philosophies, as Petrucciani recalls, can 'be very different with regard to the degree of 'distance' they take in relation to the political reality of their time' (2003, pp.14–15). Kant's republicanism, for example, as I mentioned earlier, can be seen as an attempt to correct the given political order, while maintaining its essential characteristics (for example the State form). Other political philosophies, however, such as Marx's revolutionary communism, champion the creation of a different world, in radical contrast with the present one. Philosophies such as Hegel's, on the other hand, can be read as a mere validation of the status quo, as Marx's critique argues. Petrucciani calls the philosophies of the first type 'critical', those of the second type 'utopian', and those of the third type 'apologetic'. According to his classifications, critical political philosophies are, therefore, normative philosophies. This definition, however, does not apply to queer philosophies. The criticism carried out by queer philosophies does not usually entail the elaboration of fully fledged programmes aiming at reforming existing forms of power or replacing them entirely in order to achieve a utopian condition. Queer philosophies are, for the most part, critical philosophies without a programmatic dimension, but with radical intentions that expose them to the risk of being judged as factually aporetic. Just as is the case when he goes about defining the concept of power, Petrucciani favours a 'canonical' vision of political philosophy in his classification of normative political philosophies. However, in order to understand queer theories it is necessary to embrace a heterodox point of view that will allow us to discern between the normative critical theories discussed by Petrucciani and other critical theories, which can't be a subset of normative theories, but constitute a third approach to political philosophy, different from the normative as well as the realistic one, although it is connected to, and sometimes overlaps, both.

What is critique then, according to this view? I will answer this question by quoting Foucault, who in a conference in 1978 argued that critique is 'the art of voluntary inservitude, of reflective indocility' (1996, p.304), 'the art of not being governed or the art of not being governed like that and at this price' (p.303). According to Foucault, the aim of political critical philosophies is not to elaborate normative criteria on the basis of which to amend the status quo or to plan a radically alternative form of government, but to expose the arbitrary character of normative criteria that current forms of power use to justify their actions. Thus understood, critical political philosophies present a destructive dimension unaccompanied by a constructive one. Their function is to denounce 'social pathologies' – to use a term favoured by the critical social theories of Theodor Adorno, Max Horkheimer and Herbert Marcuse – and not to find a remedy or to develop criteria of normalcy. For this reason, they are exposed to the easy criticism of normative philosophers, who can accuse them of being crypto-normative (Fraser, 1981; Habermas, 1987, p.276), that is, of not exposing the values that underpin their judgements. This is a legitimate objection. However, it remains true that for Foucault critique does not need other justification than the will – at times the necessity – to resist power, here and now.[19]

In the 'most canonical philosophical political tradition', as Petrucciani calls it, both normative and realistic philosophies ultimately endorse the point of view of those who exercise or would like to exercise power effectively, legitimately or fairly. Critical political philosophies, instead, approach power from the perspective of those who are governed and oppressed by a power that is felt as intolerable – the perspective of those belonging to subaltern classes and 'races',[20] to the 'second sex',[21] and to so-called 'sexual minorities'.[22] Critical political theories share with realistic theories the disillusioned awareness that the political dimension is marked by conflicts that cannot always be overcome. In other words, they have no ambition to pacify social conflict by way of devising universal solutions but recognise and declare their own partiality.

Critical philosophers are militant intellectuals, who, far from defending an ideal of neutrality in their knowledge, take a stand in the political struggles of their time. Foucault would not have written what he did if the 1960s and 1970s had not been traversed by the radical demands of left-wing movements against the abuses of psychiatry, against prison abuses and against an oppressive traditional sexual morality. Critical political theories are often born in times of political crisis, within and in relation to social movements, and seek their interlocutors in such movements, rather than in academia. This applies in particular, as I will show later, to queer theories, which would be unthinkable without the queer movements behind them.

In conclusion, using some of the definitions provided so far, we can describe queer theories as critical political philosophies that deploy the perspective of sexual minorities and denounce as arbitrary, illegal and intolerable the very regime that produces them as minoritarian in the first place. These philosophies do not necessarily offer solutions or alternatives, but mostly leave to social movements and individual activists the task of developing and experimenting with them. They constitute a broad field of research, and now a tradition,[23] in which different voices and opinions debate the relationship between power and sexuality, using the method of the best argument and at the same time inventing new concepts and assigning new meanings to terms that already exist (starting from the term 'queer'). Their political critique privileges 'micro-physical' (Foucault), rather than institutionalised, notions of power, according to which power isn't exclusively exercised from above but pervades society as a whole, and even individuals. The workings of a power so conceived are not limited to law, prohibition or violence, but are also at play in the production of social relations and subjectivities. In sum, queer philosophies are 'ontologies of actuality'. They do not claim to solve universal questions and they do not legislate on the basis of an abstract idea of humanity, as though philosophers could take on God's point of view. On the contrary, they articulate questions from within the specific position that the philosopher occupies in time and space, without striving for totality. They are therefore also 'ontologies of ourselves', which cannot avoid interrogating the ways in which sexual subjectivities are produced in the present: since when and how, for example, have we learned to reduce the multiplicity of expressions of human sexuality to binary oppositions such as women and men, transgender and cisgender, heterosexual and homosexual? And since when and how have we learned to fashion our personal and public identities in line with these categories? In the third chapter I will provide some examples of queer theories, distinguishing between three different approaches within the wide-ranging debate that presently characterises this field of research, which I indicate as 'revolutionary Freudo-Marxism', 'radical constructivism' and 'anti-social theories'. In the next chapter, however, I will first try to answer the questions mentioned above.

Notes

1 *Bad Education* is, not surprisingly, the title of the latest work announced by queer theorist Lee Edelman, yet to be published. For the moment, see Edelman (2017).
2 'For if you kill me, [Socrates tells the Athenians in his *Apology*], you will not readily find my like – one who, who … "settles" on the city (grotesque as this simile sounds) as a gadfly settles on a horse that is tall and thoroughbred, but somewhat sluggish and in need of being aroused. Such am I; and it is God who has given me to Athens to rouse you and urge you on and reproach you; nor do I ever cease from settling upon you at every point all day long. Such another man you will not easily discover; and if you listen to me to me, you will spare my life' (Plato, 1929, 30–31a, p.80).
3 Translators' note: the translations into English of this and other texts quoted, which have not been officially translated into English, are by the translators of this book, M. Baldo and E. Basile.
4 On the concept of action, see Arendt (1958). On the political concept of evil, and on the different possibilities of thematising it, see Forti (2014).
5 We refer here to the texts published in an Italian collection of Foucault's writings, titled *Microfisica del potere* (1977).
6 For a feminist critique of this passage see Cavarero (2002, p.159; 2009, p.23).
7 See Rich (1976). See also Cavarero (2016).
8 After all Simone de Beauvoir did argue that 'one is not born, but rather becomes, woman' (2009, p.330).
9 Translators' note: this is the first of many instances in which Bernini uses the phrase 'dispositivo di sessualità' (elsewhere 'dispositivo di potere'), where 'dispositivo' translates Foucault's notion of 'dispositif'. In English translations of Foucault's work, the term has been rendered in multiple ways, as 'device', 'deployment' and 'apparatus' and, far more rarely, 'dispositive'. While 'apparatus' seems to have become the most commonly used translation of 'dispositif', contemporary Foucaultian scholars have increasingly questioned such choice, and have made persuasive arguments

for reintroducing the old English word 'dispositive'. In particular, Raffnsøe et al. (2014) argue that 'dispositive', despite being obsolete 'covers almost the same semantic field as the French word', which includes a common etymological relation to the 'Latin verb *dis-pōnăre* [*sic*]' which means '"to set in order", "to arrange or array", "to dispose", or "to form"' (p.277). According to Raffnsøe et al., 'these older connotations of the word *dispositive* are relevant for understanding its significance in Foucault's body of work' (p.277). Raffnsøe's and other scholars' explanation of the value of reintroducing the ancient English word to translate Foucault's 'dispositif', convinced us that 'dispositive' was the best way to translate Bernini's extensive use of this Foucaultian term. For a more detailed discussion of 'dispositif' and its translation, see the 'Translators' preface'.

10 The concepts of 'biopolitics' and 'device of sexuality' will be clarified in the third chapter. See also Bernini (2008).

11 The Maastricht Treaty was signed on 7 February 1992, and Habermas was one of the most influential philosophical voices in the debate on the idea of Europe, which preceded and followed it. See, for example, Habermas (1992, 2001).

12 For an Italian example of this see Sini (2007). Jacques Rancière, on the other hand, insists on the absence of foundation in political philosophy and on the impossibility of justifying political action based on truth. On the contrary, for him politics is constituted by radical disagreement ('mésentente'). See Rancière (1999).

13 Translators's note: the English published translation of Foucault's expression reads 'ontologies of present reality' (2010, p.21). This translation, however, does not capture the full semantic range neither of the French 'actualité', nor of 'attualità', which is the Italian translation of Foucault's expression, and which Bernini uses extensively. 'Actualité' and 'attualità' cover both the notion of 'present reality' and the more philosophical and dynamic idea of what becomes actual in the unfolding of events. In a long email conversation with the author, we discussed the pros and cons of using the English word 'actuality' instead of 'present reality' to translate 'attualità'. While the English word 'actuality' has the advantage of recalling the philosophical dimension of 'attualità', it is very rarely used as a synonym for 'current times' or 'the present moment'. Accordingly, we have used the word 'actuality' to translate 'attualità' where Bernini underscores the philosophical concept of actuality as the dynamic interaction and actualisation of power through the subject and of the subject through power. Where the word 'attualità' refers more obviously to the concept of current events or current reality, we have opted to use 'the present', 'present reality' or 'current times'. Finally, where Bernini discusses Deleuze and Guattari's distinction between the 'actual' (Fr. 'actuel') and the 'present', the Italian 'attualità' has been rendered as 'the actual'.

14 Foucault's works appear often in the guise of historical research, as their titles and subtitles suggest: *History of Madness* (1961); *Discipline*

and Punish: The Birth of the Prison (1975); *The Will to Knowledge: History of Sexuality Volume I* (1976).

15 Translators's note: for Kant, as for the majority of classical philosophers, the philosopher is understood as male, which justifies our use of the male pronoun in this passage.

16 See endnote 1 above.

17 See chapter XV of Machiavelli (1513).

18 Hobbes borrows the famous expression 'homo homini lupus' from Plautus' *Asinaria* (Macci Plauti Comoediae Superst. XX, Amstelodami 1630, p.63: 'Lupus est homo homini, non homo, quom qualis sit non nouit'). The male sex is here conceived, once again, as the universal representative of humanity.

19 In *Notes toward a Performative Theory of Assembly* (2015), Judith Butler admits that her thought has a normative character when she responds to similar objections. The normativity that she theorises, however, is 'weak', 'doubtful' and non-prescriptive; it coincides with the desire (typical of critical theories) for a world where it would be possible to loosen the grip of norms on the life of minority subjects, and to break away from normality: 'The political aspiration of this analysis, perhaps its normative aim, is to let the lives of gender and sexual minorities become more possible and more livable, for bodies that are gender nonconforming as well as those that conform too well (and at a high cost) to be able to breathe and move more freely in public and private spaces, as well as all those zones that cross and confound those two. Of course, the theory of gender performativity that I formulated never prescribed which gender performances were right, or more subversive, and which were wrong, and reactionary, even when it was clear that I valued the breakthrough of certain kinds of gender performances into public space, free of police brutality, harassment, criminalization, and pathologization. The point was precisely to relax the coercive hold of norms on gendered life – which is not the same as transcending or abolishing all norms – for the purpose of living a more livable life. This last is a normative view not in the sense that it is a form of normality, but only in the sense that it represents a view of the world as it should be. Indeed, the world as it should be would have to safeguard breaks with normality, and offer support and affirmation for those who make those breaks' (pp.32–33).

20 I use the term 'race', within quotation marks, not to indicate a natural given, but those political processes that racialise one human group by making it subordinate to another. See the classic work by Fanon (1952); Mbembe (2013); and also, the recent work of journalistic style, by T.N. Coates (2015).

21 For Simone de Beauvoir (*The Second Sex*), woman is 'the second sex' because it is understood in a relationship of subordination to men. Furthermore, for Luce Irigaray (1985), woman belongs to a 'sex which is not one'. Translators' note: In Italian, Bernini uses 'sesso femminile'

['the female sex'] and 'sesso maschile' ['the male sex'] for what we translated as 'woman' and 'men'. By translating 'sesso femminile' with 'woman' and 'sesso maschile' with 'men', we followed current English translations of de Beauvoir and Irigaray, who in any case regularly use the word 'femme' ['woman'] in their writing. This said, the English feminist tradition of marking a strong distinction between 'sex' and 'gender' (where sex belongs to biology and gender belongs to culture) is less pronounced in the tradition of Italian feminist discourse, where using 'sesso' may straddle both 'sex' (nature) and 'gender' (culture). This is because the term 'gender', understood in the Anglophone feminist tradition since the late 1960s as the social construction of sexual differences, was imported into Italian through translation only towards the late 1980s (see Di Cori, 1987). The term was translated with the word 'genere', which already existed in Italian to designate grammatical gender. However, according to Di Cori (1987), acceptance of 'genere' as the best translation of 'gender' proved difficult, not only because of the narrow grammatical meaning accorded to 'genere', but mostly because the term, especially in connection to the word 'studies' (as in 'studi di genere'), was perceived to be anonymous, and not to recognise the history of women in the Italian intellectual scene. The Italian term 'sesso' [sex] is thus still prevalently used for both sex and gender and its use has been reinforced by the Italian feminism of difference, which tended to use sex as a synonym of gender (see d'Amelia, 2000).

22 I use here the term 'minority' not in a numerical but in a political sense. I consider belonging to a minority not a mere statistic, but the result of the production of social standards which define what counts as the norm, and therefore who is included in, and who is excluded from the majority.

23 These philosophies may even constitute a canon, albeit an 'inverse' one according to the ironic title of E.A.G. Arfini and C. Lo Iacono's anthology, *Canone inverso. Antologia di teoria queer* (2012).

References

Arendt, H. (1951) *The Origins of Totalitarianism*. New York: Harcourt, Brace & Company.

Arendt, H. (1958) *The Human Condition*. Chicago: University of Chicago Press.

Arendt, H. (1963) *Eichmann in Jerusalem: A Report on the Banality of Evil*. New York: Viking Press.

Arfini, E.A.G. and Lo Iacono, C. (eds) (2012) *Canone inverso. Antologia di teoria queer*. Pisa: Edizioni ETS.

Aristotle (1997) *Topics*. Translated by R. Smith. Oxford: Clarendon Press.

Bernini, L. (2008) *Le pecore e il pastore. Critica, politica, etica nel pensiero di Michel Foucault*. Napoli: Liguori.

Bobbio, N. (1999) *Teoria generale della politica*. Torino: Einaudi.

Butler, J. (2015) *Notes Toward a Performative Theory of Assembly*. Cambridge, MA: Harvard University Press.

Cavarero, A. (2002) *Stately Bodies: Literature, Philosophy and the Question of Gender*. Translated by R. de Lucca. Ann Arbor: University of Michigan Press.

Cavarero, A. (2009) *Horrorism: Naming Contemporary Violence*. Translated by W. McCuaig. New York: Columbia University Press.

Cavarero, A. (2016) *Inclinations: A Critique of Rectitude*. Translated by A. Minervini and A. Sitze. Stanford: Stanford University Press.

Coates, T.N. (2015) *Between the World and Me*. Melbourne: The Text Publishing.

D'Amelia, M. (2000) '"Genere" and "Sesso" in Italian Language and Feminism' in R. Braidotti and E. Vonk (eds), *The Making of European Women's Studies: A Work in Progress Report on Curriculum Development and Related Issues*. Utrecht: ATHENA, pp.83–89.

De Beauvoir, S. (2009) *The Second Sex*. Translated by C. Borde and S. Malovany-Chevallier. New York: Vintage.

Deleuze, G. and Guattari, F. (1994) *What is Philosophy?* Translated by H. Tomlinson and G. Burchell. New York: Columbia University Press.

Di Cori, P. (1987) 'Dalla storia delle donne ad una storia di genere', *Rivista di storia contemporanea* 4: 548–559.

Edelman, L. (2017) 'Learning Nothing: Bad Education', *Differences* 28(1): 124–173.

Fanon, F. (1952) *Black Skin, White Masks*. Translated by C.L. Markmann (2008). London: Pluto Press.

Forti, S. (2014) *New Demons: Rethinking Power and Evil Today*. Translated by Z. Hanafi. Stanford: Stanford University Press.

Foucault, M. (1961) *History of Madness*. Translated by J. Khalfa and J. Murphy (2006). New York: Routledge.

Foucault, M. (1975) *Discipline and Punish: The Birth of the Prison*. Translated by A. Sheridan (1995). New York: Vintage Books.

Foucault, M. (1976) *The Will to Knowledge: History of Sexuality*, vol. 1 (1998). London: Penguin Books.

Foucault, M. (1977) *Microfisica del potere*. Turin: Einaudi.

Foucault, M. (1982) 'The Subject and Power', *Critical Inquiry* 8(4): 777–795.

Foucault, M. (1996) 'What Is Critique?' in J. Schmidt (ed.), *What Is Enlightenment? Eighteenth Century Answers and Twentieth Century Questions*. Berkeley: University of California Press, pp.382–398.

Foucault, M. (2008) *Le Gouvernement de soi et des autres: Cours au Collège de France. 1982–1983*. Paris: Seuil/Gallimard.

Foucault, M. (2010) 'Lecture of 5 January 1983', in F. Gros (ed.), *The Government of Self and Others: Lectures at the Collège de France 1982–1983*. Translated by G. Burchell. London: Palgrave Macmillan.

Fraser, N. (1981) 'Foucault on Modern Power: Empirical Insight and Normative Confusions', *Praxis International* 3: 272–287.

Habermas, J. (1987) *The Philosophical Discourse of Modernity*. Translated by F.D. Lawrence. Cambridge, MA: MIT Press.

Habermas, J. (1989) *The Structural Transformation of the Public Sphere: An Inquiry into a Category of Bourgeois Society*. Translated by T. Burger and F. Lawrence. Cambridge, MA: MIT Press.

Habermas, J. (1992) 'Citizenship and National Identity: Some Reflections on the Future of Europe', *Praxis International* 12(1): 1–19.

Habermas, J. (1998) *On the Pragmatics of Communication*. Ed. M. Cooke. Cambridge, MA: MIT Press.

Habermas, J. (2001) 'Why Does Europe Need a Constitution?', *Documents* 56(4): 24–40.

Hegel, G.W. (1820) *Elements of the Philosophy of Right*. Ed. A.W. Wood. Translated by N.B Nisbet (2003). Cambridge: Cambridge University Press.

Hobbes, T. (1642) *On the Citizen*. Ed. R. Tuck and M. Silverthorne (1998). Cambridge: Cambridge University Press.

Hobbes, T. (1651) *Leviathan, Or, the Matter, Forme and Power of a Common Wealth Ecclesiasticall and Civil*. Ed. N. Malcolm (2012). Oxford: Clarendon Press.

Irigaray, L. (1985) *This Sex Which Is Not One*. Translated by G. Gill. Ithaca, NY: Cornell University Press.

Kant, I. (1758) 'The Contest of the Faculties, Part 2 The Question Renewed: Is Humankind Continually Improving?' in P. Kleingeld (ed.), *Toward Perpetual Peace and Other Writings on Politics, Peace and History*. Translated by D.L. Colclasure (2006c). Binghamton: Yale University Press, pp.150–163.

Kant, I. (1781) *Critique of Pure Reason*. Translated by M. Weigelt and M. Muller (2008). London: Penguin Classics.

Kant, I. (1784) 'An Answer to the Question: What is Enlightenment?' in P. Kleingeld (ed.), *Toward Perpetual Peace and Other Writings on Politics, Peace and History*. Translated by D.L. Colclasure (2006b). Binghamton: Yale University Press, pp.17–23.

Kant, I. (1784) 'Idea for a Universal History from a Cosmopolitan Perspective' in P. Kleingeld (ed.), *Toward Perpetual Peace and Other Writings on Politics, Peace and History*. Translated by D.L. Colclasure (2006d). Binghamton: Yale University Press, pp.3–16.

Kant, I. (1790) *Critique of Judgment*. Translated by J. Creed Meredith (2007). Oxford: Oxford University Press.

Kant, I. (1795) 'Toward Perpetual Peace: A Philosophical Sketch' in P. Kleingeld (ed.), *Toward Perpetual Peace and Other Writings on Politics, Peace and History.* Translated by D.L. Colclasure (2006a). Binghamton: Yale University Press, pp.68–109.

Kant, I. (1800) *Lectures on Logic.* Ed. and translated by M. Young (1992). Cambridge: Cambridge University Press.

Machiavelli, N. (1513) *The Prince.* Translated by H.C. Mansfield (1985). Chicago and London: University of Chicago Press.

Marx, K. (1843) *Critique of Hegel's Philosophy of Right.* Translated by J. O'Malley (1970). Oxford: Oxford University Press.

Marx, K. (1867) *Capital: Critique of Political Economy Vol. I.* Translated by B. Fowkes (1990). London: Penguin Classics.

Marx, K. (1885) *Capital: Critique of Political Economy Vol. II.* Translated by D. Fernbach (1992). London: Penguin Classics.

Marx, K. (1894) *Capital: Critique of Political Economy Vol. III.* Translated by D. Fernbach (1992). London: Penguin Classics.

Mbembe, A. (2013) *Critique de la raison négre.* Paris: La Découverte.

Petrucciani, S. (2003) *Modelli di filosofia politica.* Torino: Einaudi.

Plato (1929) *The Apology of Socrates.* Translated and edited by E.H. Blakeney. London: The Scholartis Press.

Plato (2005) *The Republic.* Translated by R.E. Allen. New Haven: Yale University Press.

Raffnsøe, S., Gudmand-Hòyer, M. and Thaning, M.S. (2014) 'Foucault's Dispositive: The Perspicacity of Dispositive Analytics in Organizational Research', *Organization* 23(2): 272–298.

Rancière, J. (1999) *Dis-Agreement: Politics and Philosophy.* Translated by J. Rose. Minneapolis: University of Minnesota Press.

Rich, A. (1976) *Of Woman Born: Motherhood as Experience and Institution.* New York: Norton.

Schmitt, C. (1932) *The Concept of the Political.* Translated by G. Schwab (1996). Chicago: University of Chicago Press.

Sini, C. (2007) *Eracle al bivio. Semiotica e filosofia.* Torino: Bollati Boringhieri.

Strauss, Leo (1989) 'What Is Political Philosophy' in H. Gildin (ed.), *An Introduction to Political Philosophy: Ten Essays by Leo Strauss.* Detroit: Wayne State University Press, pp.3–58.

Weber, M. (1946) 'Politics as Vocation' in H.H. Gerth and C. Wright-Mills (eds), *From Max Weber: Essays in Sociology.* Oxford: Oxford University Press, pp.77–128.

2 An exercise in queer critique

How does sexuality function?

Revolutionary Freudo-Marxism, radical constructivism and anti-social theories constitute three typologies of queer philosophy, three styles of critical theory that investigate in different ways the relationship between politics and sexuality from the point of view of sexual minorities. As I will show in the following pages, these three styles depart from one another primarily on the basis of which one among sexuality's many dimensions they choose as a privileged viewpoint on power. In Mario Mieli's Freudo-Marxism, for example, sexuality is interpreted as *sexual desire*, on the liberation of which the subject's own liberation depends; in the radical constructivism of Michel Foucault and Judith Butler, sexuality is understood above all as *sexual identity* shaped by norms that the subject can oppose resistance to; and, finally, in the antisocial theories of Leo Bersani and Lee Edelman, sexuality is understood as a *sexual drive* that dissolves the subject through jouissance. When applied to sexuality, the 'what is' question that inaugurates philosophy leads us then straight to the heart of the queer debate. Before engaging in this debate, however, we need to adopt not only an appropriate 'vocabulary', but also an appropriate 'grammar', questioning the terms and rules of our pre-understanding of sexuality.

This second chapter, therefore, won't attempt to answer the question 'what is sexuality?', but the question 'how does sexuality work?'. That is, what are the concepts and criteria through which we represent and describe ourselves and others as sexual subjects? Before considering the different ontologies of sexuality elaborated by queer theories, I will therefore attempt to operate an 'ontology of actuality' which is also a critical ontology of ourselves, endorsing for the moment Foucault's constructivist perspective. That is, I will consider sexuality as a complex normative system, which is the precipitate and condensed effect of an extended history of different forms of knowledge that produced our present sexual identities. The question then, 'how does sexuality work?', isn't sufficient yet to explain the full scope of the next pages. Thus, the question I will try to address is, more precisely: 'how does sexuality, *understood as a dispositive of power*, work *today*?'.

2.1 Sex, gender and sexual orientation

In 2015, SIPSIS (Italian Society of Psychotherapy for the Study of Sexual Identities) responded to the more than twenty-year-long Catholic Church's campaign against the spread of the concept of gender (against what it dubbed as 'gender ideology'),[1] by publishing an informative guide, in line with the prevailing international medical-psychological knowledge on the topic.[2] In the last chapter of the guide, authors Federico Ferrari, Enrico M. Ragaglia and Paolo Rigliano (2015) give an account of what they call 'the transgender galaxy' (p.45), in which they also include the intersex condition. It is symptomatic, however, that their text opens with the presentation of three pairs of opposite concepts, sex, gender and sexual orientation, which de facto exclude intersex and transgender identities[3] from the sphere of thinkable. These are indeed the three binary criteria that are used throughout the world by most psychiatrists, psychologists, sexologists and legal systems in order to define and classify sexual identities. The three authors argue that:

> Sex is defined as the sexed body, determined by the set of specific physical and biological traits, which, within the same species, distinguish males and females *on the basis of their different reproductive functions*. Gender, instead, is understood by the world scientific community as the set of differences between men and women, which different societies construct from the differences between male and female bodies ... Gender therefore concerns those socio-cultural aspects which, in different ways from culture to culture and with different degrees of obligation, make it possible to identify male individuals as men

and female individuals as women. Such differences between
men and women are mediated by symbols, habits, norms, and
are sustained and continually recreated by collective rituals,
social practices, individual behaviour.

(pp.8–9, italics added)

Gender, then, is presented in the SIPSIS guide as the socio-psycho-
cultural counterpart of sex. Sex refers to the biological male and
female body insofar as it is in charge of 'the reproductive function'
(p.9), while gender refers to the subject's sense of self. That is,
gender has to do with our identification as male or female depend-
ing on what the society we belong to recognises as proper to males
and females. For example, a male who likes to regularly wear
makeup, a skirt and high heels is unlikely to be perceived by our
society as 'fully a man'.

The third factor determining sexual identity, according to the
three authors mentioned above, is sexual orientation, which 'refers
to the emotional, affective and erotic attraction toward members of
the opposite sex, of the same sex or of both sexes (according to
which we can identify as heterosexual, homosexual or bisexual)'
(p.6). Unlike gender identity, they specify:

[sexual orientation] is not about the shape of the self, but about
the shape and the sexual image of the other, and therefore
about the relationship with the other. Given these premises, it
is clear that a homosexual person who happily embraces their
identity does not deny the existence of men or women. A
homosexual woman, for example, feels like a woman, is
attracted to other women, but this does not mean that she
intrinsically hates men.

(p.11)

For contemporary psychology, therefore, the sexual orientation of a
person defines the direction of their desires and does not interfere
with their gender identity. In the case of homosexuality, and even
bisexuality, the binary understanding of the sexes – that is, the
division of human species into males and females – is not questioned. A gay man fully identifies with the male gender he is also
attracted to; a lesbian does the same with the female gender. A

bisexual person also identifies with the gender corresponding to their sex, and their attraction to both genders does not call into question the binary character of sexual orientation itself. Bisexuality is not a third sexual orientation, but the sum of the other two.

Ferrari et al.'s insistence on the division of the human species into males and females as an unquestionable given is explained by their need to respond to the Catholic campaign according to which Gender Studies, Queer Theories and Contemporary Psychology are associated with a dangerous 'theory', or 'ideology', aimed at erasing 'sexual difference'. Such insistence, however, is not merely a rhetorical device, but reflects the theoretical premises that regulate the actual functioning of contemporary sexuality, understood as a system of classification and as a dispositive of power. In the last chapter of the SIPSIS guide on the 'transgender galaxy', it appears that the binary distinctions concerning sex (male and female), gender (man and woman) and sexual orientation (heterosexual and homosexual, which may add up in bisexuality) are not sufficient to account for the complexity of human bodily and sexual identity formations. Yet, in the first chapters the three authors dwell uncritically on the criteria that still define nowadays the 'standards' of sexuality. These authors are, after all, in good company: not only psychological, but also medical, biological and legal disciplines nowadays are aware of the existence of at least ten criteria for classifying the sexuality of human beings, which can produce configurations that diverge from the single distinction between male and female. Despite such knowledge, however, in almost all cases these disciplines continue to make exclusive use of the binary classification.

For example, when Ferrari et al. – who define sex as a function of reproduction and thus of heterosexual intercourse – write that 'from a biological perspective belonging to the male or female sex ... is defined on the basis of sexual chromosomes, hormones, external and internal genitalia, and on the resulting overall structure of the body' (p.5), they are attributing to the male-female binary five factors that are actually independent from one another. Furthermore, they are assuming the existence of a consequentiality and a coherence between them that is not always present – and they are forgetting to mention a sixth factor. In fact, there are at least six factors that determine biological sex and they can't be exclusively reduced to the difference between male and female. Here they are:

1   Sexual chromosomes: in addition to the standard configurations of male (XY) and female (XX), there are other configurations, such as XXY, X0, XX-XY (which contemporary medicine classifies respectively as Klinefelter syndrome, Turner syndrome and sexual mosaicism).

2   Sex hormones: female (oestrogen) and male (androgen) hormones are actually present in different percentages in all human beings, and their production and absorption during pregnancy, childhood and after adolescence can produce physical appearances (called 'sexual phenotypes'[4]) typically feminine or masculine, or atypical appearances in relation to standards of femininity and masculinity.

3   External genitalia: in this case too, besides the scrotum and penis, and the vulva and clitoris, there are atypical organs with respect to masculine and feminine standards. For example, there are erectile organs of intermediate size and appearance between the penis and the clitoris, which medicine often insists on defining as 'micropenises' or 'hypertrophic clitorises'.

4   Internal genitalia: contrary to masculine and feminine standards, not only the vagina, the uterus and the ovaries, but also the testicles can be found inside the abdomen. Moreover, not all vaginas are connected to a uterus and not all are deep enough to enable the penetration of a medium-size erect penis.

5   What Ferrari et al. call the 'overall body conformation', which is often signified by the expressions 'secondary sex characteristics' or 'sexual phenotype': the presence or absence of the breasts; of the Adam's apple; of the beard, the tone of the voice; the distribution of body fat; the muscular structure; the thickness and the distribution of hairs; the width of hips and shoulders, etc. All these elements can obviously combine with one another in ways that differ from given standards of the masculine and the feminine.

6   The gonads, which the three authors forget to mention: these include not only the testicles and the ovaries, but also the ovotestis, composed of mixed testicular and ovarian tissue.

For each of these factors, therefore, there are intermediate formations, or formations that are altogether other than masculine or feminine. In addition, as I will explain further below, these factors can combine into configurations that contradict given standards of masculinity and femininity. However, in the SIPSIS guide intersexuality is only mentioned in the last chapter, as an exception confirming the rule of the binary sex/gender system, which is illustrated in the first chapter.

A similar observation can be made with regard to the concept of gender, which Ferrari et al. present as the translation of the two sexes in the domains of psychology, society and culture. However, in the last chapter, they also take into consideration gender identifications that contradict the sex assigned at birth, and gender identifications which are neither male or female but in-between. The three authors are also well aware that at least three different factors contribute to the making of gender, which – again – may combine in ways that are not consistent with standards of masculinity and femininity. These factors are:

1   Gender identity: that is, the feeling of belonging to a socially recognisable category of people; the subject's own identification as a cisgender man or woman (i.e. someone who identifies with the gender corresponding to their biological sex) or as a transgender person (i.e. someone who identifies with the gender opposite to their biological sex, or with a gender in-between male and female); gender fluid (i.e. someone who sometimes identifies as male, sometimes as female); gender questioning (i.e. someone who is questioning their gender identity); agender (neither male nor female); genderqueer or genderfuck (i.e. someone who consciously and explicitly confronts standards of masculinity and femininity).
2   Gender role: that is, the external presentation of gender according to social conventions, which may be male, female or androgynous.
3   Legal gender: that is, the gender marker that appears in birth registers and in official documents. While one's gender identity, gender role and legal gender can align with one another, they don't necessarily have to. Gender expression can thus encompass a wide range of possibilities, as many as the outcomes of the potential combinations between gender identity, gender role and legal gender. Also, they can remain unchanged over time or change over the course of one's own lifetime. And yet, despite

being aware of all of this, contemporary psychology keeps reflexively using gender as a binary concept that mirrors sexual difference and has no other options beyond the exclusive alternative of masculine and feminine.

4   For the three authors of the SIPSIS guide, this binarism isn't challenged either by the last of the sexual identity criteria that I will now examine: sexual orientation. In their view, homosexual, bisexual and heterosexual people are cisgender, that is, they adhere fully to the gender identity assigned to them at birth. However, upon a closer examination, it becomes clear that the sexual orientation category reveals some inconsistencies in the sex-gender classification system, even more so if we take into account the other factors that determine the sexual identity of a person. First of all, should sexual orientation be established on the basis of someone's gender or of someone's sex? And should the sex or the gender be that of the person concerned, or that of the sex and gender of the people to whom that person is attracted? And if we privilege sex as the determining factor, which sex exactly? Do genitalia count more than secondary sex traits? For example, shall we define the female partner of a transgender woman who has penetrative sex with her (with her penis) as a lesbian or as a straight woman? To give another example, on the basis of what criteria should we define the sexual orientation of an intersex person and of their partners? And what is the sexual orientation of two intersex people forming a couple? If, on the other hand, we choose gender as a determinant for sexual orientation, how should we define the sexual orientation of a transgender person who doesn't fully identify with either the male or the female gender? The sole distinction between homosexuals and heterosexuals is not sufficient to account for cases like these, as well as for others. There are people, for example, who call themselves pansexual, as their desire is detached from both sex and gender. Moreover, there are people who define themselves as asexual, insofar as they lack sexual desire altogether or have 'weak' sexual desire towards others.[5]

In sum, the thesis that gays and lesbians fully adhere to the gender corresponding to the one assigned to them at birth, besides the fact that it does not account for the existence of transgender lesbian women and transgender gay men, erases gender-non-con-forming experiences and behaviours that characterise the experiences of many cisgender gay men and cisgender lesbian women, and thus the phenomenon of female masculinities and male femininities (Halberstam, 1998). It is not uncommon, for example, for children and youth who later in life will embrace a gay identity to be bullied because they are judged 'effeminate' by their classmates, and that the discrimination and violence they have suffered might estrange them from the gender they are supposed to perform, based on the sex assigned to them at birth. If gender, as Ferrari et al. (2015) claim, is a psycho-socio-cultural construct, it could also be argued that in many contemporary societies, especially in large cities where there are substantial gay and lesbian communities (with entertainment venues, associations and dedicated services), the terms 'gay' and 'lesbian' have come to signify not only preferences related to the object of desire, but fully recognisable social identities, even perhaps actual genders in their own right.

The 'sex-gender-sexual orientation' classification system is therefore imperfect, unsatisfactory and contradictory, and produces ideal types ('Man', 'Woman', but also 'Heterosexual', 'Homosexual'), which are sometimes very far removed from the life experiences of those whom this system is supposed to describe. How is it possible, then, that every contemporary treatise on sexuality, as the SIPSIS guide also shows, seems unable to do away with this classification system? And how is it possible that medical, psychological and legal discourses, despite being aware of the multidimensionality and complexity of human beings' sexual identities, are still unable to reject the standards of sexuality that are the product of such system? In order to answer these questions, I will adopt, as previously mentioned, the historical-constructivist methodology inaugurated by Foucault (1976). In other words, I will consider sexuality as a properly modern dispositive of power: that is, as a complex interweaving of conventions, norms, practices, knowledge, whose effect is the governance of bodies, behaviours and subjectivities through the definition and imposition of sexual identities. I will also argue that in contemporary societies – through psychiatry, psychology, medicine, law, culture, common sense – the binary sex/gender system[6] acts on our sexual identities as a 'biopolitical agent',[7] which reduces the complexity of the factors involved in the definition of sexual identity by imposing *rigid binary choices between two terms* equally at the level of sex (male or female), of gender (man or woman) and of sexual orientation (heterosexual or homosexual). In this interpretative perspective, the three standard criteria of sexuality thus emerge as vectors of power that render some expressions of sexuality unintelligible, whereas others are made intelligible only by means of specific arrangements of the three criteria themselves: i.e. cisgender men, either heterosexual, homosexual (gay) or bisexual; cisgender women, either heterosexual, homosexual (lesbians) or bisexual; transgender women (or transgender mtf, that is male to female), either heterosexual, homosexual (lesbians) or bisexual; transgender men (or transgender ftm, that is female to male) either heterosexual, homosexual (gay) or bisexual ...

These identities have been theorised by psychiatry and sexology fairly recently. In *La volonté de savoir*, Foucault argues that the modern concept of homosexuality was introduced in 1869, in Carl Friedrich Otto Westphal's (cited in Foucault, 1976, p.59) article 'Die conträre Sexualempfindung'. However, on this point, we must disagree with his analysis and postpone the birth of sexuality's contemporary dispositive by about eighty years. The category of 'contrary sexual feeling', through which Westphal refers to homosexuality in the article quoted by Foucault, does not allow us to differentiate between what today we call homosexuality and what we call transgenderism, as Westphal subsumes the two concepts within the same category, understanding them as inversions of male and female elements of the psyche.

Still in the essays of the most famous psychiatrists and sexologists of the nineteenth and early twentieth centuries, such as Richard von Krafft-Ebing's *Psychopathia sexualis*, first published in 1886, Henry Havelock Ellis's *Sexual Inversion*, first published in 1897, and David O. Cauldwell's 'Psychopathia Trans-sexualis', published in 1949, there is no clear distinction between homosexuality and transgenderism, and both are understood according to the inversion model (between the masculine and the feminine). It is only after 1953 – that is, after the publication of Henry Benjamin's (1953)[8] article 'Transvestitism and Transexualism' – that the term 'trans-sexual', already used by Cauldwell as an adjective, comes to be used as a noun to indicate a specific category of people. It is at this moment in time, then, that the identity category of the 'invert' splits into two, giving rise to two identities, the homosexual and the transsexual, and that the difference between gender identity and sexual orientation is thus conceptualised. On the other hand, the difference between sex and gender will be definitively formalised four years later, in 1957, in the article by John Money and spouses John and Joan Hampson, 'Imprinting and the Establishment of the Gender Role'.[9] From this moment onward, the classification system with which we still nowadays categorise not only homosexuality and transgenderism, but also heterosexuality and cisgenderism, and masculinity and femininity, becomes well known and established knowledge worldwide.[10]

To understand why the binary alternatives of such a system don't just drastically simplify the range of possible sexual identities, but are also vectors of power, we need to understand that in both psychiatry and law these categories, whose history I am presently outlining, have not served a merely descriptive function. On the contrary, they have served for a long time, and sometimes still serve nowadays, to establish a hierarchical order whereby only certain categories of people are acknowledged as belonging to a 'healthy', 'normal' and 'full' humanity, and thus as fully deserving of legal protection. (In Italy, for example, the Civil Unions Law approved in May 2016 denies homosexual couples access to the marriage institution, the right to be called a family[11] and the right to adoption that the Italian legal system grants to heterosexual couples).

As a first shorthand characterisation of contemporary queer theories (or rather, most of them), we can say that they follow the methodology inaugurated by Foucault and produce a 'denaturalisation' of the categories attendant to the binary sex/gender system, insofar as they insist on the fact that these are historical and normative constructs. Going back to what we stated in the previous chapter, we can therefore say that queer theories demonstrate their philosophical status because they don't hold back from confronting the truths produced by science and the norms imposed by law, but question their meaning and their legitimacy moving from an intersubjective point of view. Moreover, they demonstrate their critical status because they express the views of sexual minorities who resist the regime of truth that both defines and governs them. The transgender condition and the intersex condition, which I will now briefly address, are particularly significant vantage points for the kind of critical exercise in a queer ontology of actuality that I am proposing.

2.2 Critique of the binary sex/gender system: the transgender point of view

The *DSM* (*Diagnostic and Statistical Manual of Mental Disorders*), produced by the American Psychiatric Association, is the world's most used manual for the classification of mental disorders. First published in 1952, the textbook reached its fifth edition in 2013. Heterosexuality, unsurprisingly, has never appeared among the disorders that the textbook examines, contrary to other identities produced by the binary sex/gender system. Homosexuality was removed from the list partially in 1974, and definitively in 1987;[12] transgenderism instead is still present. Both in the manual's third edition (1980) – in which it appeared for the first time[13] – and again in the fourth edition (1994), transgenderism was referred to as either 'transsexualism' or 'gender identity disorder'.[14] This categorisation is obviously based on the norm that imposes coherence between sex and gender, and that punishes those for whom such coherence does not manifest by labelling them as 'abnormal' or 'mentally disturbed'. As of the DSM's fifth edition (2013), transgenderism has now been given the name of 'gender dysphoria'. Within thirty years, transgenderism has thus become a less severe psychiatric condition, since it does not concern a person's identity, but their mood. It is in fact understood as accompanied by depression caused by a lack of correspondence between identity and biology – a lack, however, that is not considered pathological in and of itself.

To summarise, if we follow authoritative sources of international psychiatry, we can state that: (1) at the end of the nineteenth century, homosexual and transgender people were affected by the same disorder of 'sexual inversion'; (2) in the mid-1950s it was instead 'discovered' that in fact such disorder was not one but two, which concerned, respectively, sexual orientation and gender; (3) in 1974 some homosexuals healed, followed by others in 1987, and as of 1980, all transgender people started falling seriously ill; (4) these latter remain ill to this day, although since 2013 their disorder is milder than before. Subjects born male who self-identified as women, or subjects born female who self-identified as men, suffered from a serious identity disorder up until the DSM's fifth edition; today, however, they get away with a diagnosis of dysphoria, a much milder disorder!

Throughout this curious history, it is significant that transsexual identity became fully theorised as distinct from homosexual identity in the medical field in the 1950s. The first protocols of hormonal and surgical therapies designed to make the body of one sex phenotypically resemble that of another sex were indeed developed during this period in the wake of intense experimentations. Henry Benjamin's 1953 article, 'Transvestitism and Transexualism', described the clinical case of Christin Jorgensen – born George – who is often wrongly presented as the first person to undergo the so-called sex reassignment surgery,[15] whereas she was instead one of the first public spokespersons for transgender issues. The techniques used have improved extensively over time: a transgender man (or transgender ftm) can now choose to take testosterone and/or undergo mastectomy, vaginectomy, hysterectomy, ovariectomy, phalloplasty or metoidioplasty; a transgender woman (or transgender mtf) can take testosterone blockers and oestrogens, and/or undergo additive mastoplasty, orchiectomy, penectomy, vaginoplasty, in addition to having recourse to depilation and cosmetic surgery. The possibilities provided by medicine are many – more or less invasive, more or less risky[16] – and each person should be free to personalise over time their own gender transition, based on their desires and with all the support they deem necessary, including eventually – though not prescriptively – also psychological support. On the other hand, freedom of choice for transgender people is still too often limited, not only by their own financial resources (costs associated with surgery and therapy aren't all covered by the public health system, nor are they covered in every country), but also by the protocols and laws that regulate sex change. What has happened in Italy over the last half-century, for example, is indicative of how severely the sex/gender binary can harm the self-determination of transgender people. It is also indicative, however, of how these latter have been able to challenge such binary by creating political movements, building alliances and obtaining consensus – all of which have changed and continue to change the political landscape. As the current president of the Transsexual Identity Movement (MIT), Porpora Marcasciano, recalls:

> The first case of surgical sex reassignment in Italy is that of Romina Cecconi, which was carried out in 1966 in Switzerland.

Three years later, in 1969, Cecconi was sentenced to confinement in a small town in the province of Foggia because she was
considered morally and socially dangerous. The court order
was deemed necessary by judge Vigna because of the repeated
infractions (art. 85 C.P.) concerning disguise, and of the
numerous police arrests that had earned Cecconi the title of
'habitual offender', as for Article 1. Up until the mid-1980s
Article 1 constituted for the vast majority of transgender people
a proper form of persecution, which deprived them of all sorts
of freedoms, including the freedom of movement.

(2006, p.43)[17]

Even in such an oppressive regime, transgender people found the
strength to dress the way they felt better reflected their identity, to
adjust their body to the image they had of themselves (by going
abroad, if necessary, to undergo surgery that was not practised in
Italy) and to appear in public defying the law. They were then able
to form political movements, gain public visibility,[18] gain the right
to access the medical procedures they needed and change the gender
assigned to them at birth. And their struggle is far from being over.

Law 164, which regulates sex reassignment in Italy, was adopted
on 14 April 1982 and underwent a few procedural changes in 2011.
It is a rather skeletal law, which states that a court ruling must be
used to authorise sex change. However, for more than thirty years,
its interpretation has made genital surgery a compulsory requirement for the purpose of gender change on one's birth certificate.
During this period, then, out of the at least ten criteria for sex/
gender classification previously mentioned, Italian jurisprudence has
given priority to the gender identity inscribed on the birth registry
and to the appearance of one's genitalia, establishing a direct
equivalence between the two. It has also provided a literal juridical
interpretation of the medical term 'transsexual', understood as a
person who *must* change her/his genitalia in order to have her/his
gender identity institutionally recognised. Since phalloplasty can
lead to serious complications, in the case of ftm transgender people,
the surgical obligation has been limited to removal surgery: in order
to have their name changed on the birth registry, their ability to
reproduce had to be irreversibly compromised. In Italy, therefore, a
person's gender identity has been based for a long time not on their

sense of self, but exclusively on their genitalia, either natural, surgically reconstructed or at least rendered sterile. Legally speaking, then, a man with a uterus and ovaries, or a woman with testicles and a penis, have been treated as impossible subjects. However, these subjects are actually more than possible: they exist, they define themselves as 'transgender', and they can be taken as exemplary figures of critique and resistance against the power dispositive of the sex/gender binary.[19] The term transgender did not originate in medicine, but in activism, and has spread among LGBTQI+ movements following the publication in 1992 of Leslie Feinberg's pamphlet 'Transgender Liberation'.[20]

The term has multiple meanings. First, we call transgender those people who identify with the gender opposite to that assigned to them at birth but who do not wish to undergo genital surgery. One can be transgender, for example, by dressing in the clothes associated to their desired gender; by choosing a name of their preferred gender for themselves; or by eventually taking hormones and modifying some features of their body, but without resorting to either phalloplasty or vaginoplasty. Second, transgender people can be like Leslie Feinberg themself, who, after having experimented with different gender roles throughout their life and having made their body partially resemble a male body, has embraced an identity which is neither male nor female.[21] Finally, over time, the transgender category has come to identify also those people that psychology, using a more traditional term, continues to call 'transsexuals', and who want to modify their genitalia also. 'Transgender' has thus become an umbrella term (and this is how I have mostly used it so far) that contains the whole range of possible identities for those who, born to one sex, do not feel like they belong to its corresponding gender.

The movements that prefer this term over 'transsexual' do so for several reasons: to avoid the medical and pathological connotation attached to the latter term; to underscore that surgery, for those who wish to undertake it, could be a means for expressing their *own* gender identity without having to necessarily endorse stereotypical views of gender based on coherence between gender and genitalia's appearance; to claim the specificity of the transgender identity as different from standard male and female gender identities (and not necessarily occupying a middle position between them). A few years before the term became popular, the same concept had been conveyed by Sandy Stone (2006) when she invited transsexual people to become 'posttranssexual', that is, to cease any effort to 'pass' as men and women in order to make themselves publicly 'readable' in the complexity of their paths and in the authenticity of their stories:

> I could not ask a transsexual for anything more inconceivable than to forgo passing, to be consciously 'read', to read oneself aloud – and by this troubling and productive reading, to begin to *write oneself* into the discourses by which one has been written – in effect, then, to become a (look out – dare I say it again?) posttranssexual. Still, transsexuals know that silence can be an extremely high price to pay for acceptance. I want to speak directly to the brothers and sisters who may read/'read' this and say: I ask all of us to use the strength which brought us through the effort of restructuring identity, and which has also helped us to live in silence and denial, for a revisioning of our lives. I know you feel that most of the work is behind you and that the price of invisibility is not great. But, although *individual* change is the foundation of all things, it is not the end of all things. Perhaps it's time to begin laying the ground for the next transformation.[22]
>
> (p.232)

Transgender identity is therefore, also, a political identity that challenges the sex/gender binary and encourages its transformation (it is 'posttranssexual' because it questions the way in which transsexuality was conceived based on binary logic). Its popularity has raised new awareness in LGBTQI+ movements around the world and has ended up having a significant impact also on Italian courts. In recent years, thanks to the determination of transgender people, LGBTQI+ associations and the efforts of skilled lawyers, a less restrictive interpretation of Law 164[23] has gradually taken hold. More and more often, in exceptional cases, especially in the presence of pathologies that would have made the surgery dangerous, the change of gender on the birth certificate has been granted even in the absence of genital surgery. Two important verdicts, issued respectively by the Court of Appeal in July 2015 (n. 15138, 20 July 2015) and by the Constitutional Court in November of the same year (n. 221, 5 November 2015), have definitively stated that such surgeries should be deemed unnecessary for one's change of name on the birth certificate, specifically if the person in question has already achieved a 'psychophysical balance', and that 'each person' should be free to choose 'the ways in which they want to transition, with the assistance of the doctor and other specialists'. This was an important victory, although not the final one, for Italian transgender movements. Meanwhile, pending a new law that would adhere to the most advanced international regulations,[24] in Italy the legal change of gender has to be authorised not only by the courts but also by psychologists and doctors who have to produce the evaluations required by the courts. The path is strenuous and tortuous. Indeed, the protocols established by the centres that deal with gender change impose long waiting lists and sometimes the costs for psychological certifications and legal advice are high. The transgender person has to keep their original name for a long time, even though their body is changing as a consequence of hormonal treatments and/or cosmetic surgery. In any case, they are exposed to the stigma of pathologisation, as they have to demonstrate that they 'suffer' from gender dysphoria, according to the criteria established by the DSM.[25] Finally, as I write, the two published verdicts are still too recent for me to be able to evaluate how they will be received by Italian courts. In particular, it is not clear how judges will behave in cases of individuals whose fertility has not been halted by hormonal therapies. Nevertheless, the achievements of the transgender movements in only half a century in Italy and around the world – from the confinement of Romina Cecconi to the verdicts of the Court of Appeal and the Constitutional Court that expunge the obligation of genital surgery; from the invention of the nosographic category of 'gender identity disorder' to its downgrading to the category of dysphoria – demonstrate that the sex/gender binary is not an immutable law of nature, but a historical dispositive of power, whose rules can be challenged, modified or even abolished. These observations cannot but motivate transgender people to intensify their struggle for self-determination further. As a result, they never fail to provoke discomfort and alarm among those who stand as guardians of the binary system and its fundamental norm: compulsory heterosexuality.

2.3 Critique of compulsory heterosexuality: the intersex perspective

In 2015, when SIPSIS published the guide edited by Ferrari, Ragaglia and Rigliano, the campaign of the Catholic Church against the so-called 'gender ideology' had already reached a wide audience. In December 2012, while intervening in the French debate on same-sex marriage, Pope Benedict XVI had argued that the term 'gender' underpins a dangerous philosophy according to which being male or female 'is no longer an original natural reality' dictated by God's will, and the family ceases to be a 'reality predetermined by creation' (Ratzinger, 2012).[26] His words – which in the following years were echoed by his successor Bergoglio[27] and, with some change, by the Synod of Bishops[28] – have triggered a wide and hostile reaction by traditionalist movements, which in Italy has gained significant traction.[29] In addition to same-sex marriages, Bergoglio's Church – supported by organisations of Catholic inspiration such as Manif Pour Tous Italy [Protest for All], Giuristi per la Vita [Jurists for Life], Difendiamo i nostri figli [Let's Defend Our Children], Il Popolo della famiglia [The People of the Family] and far right-wing parties such as Forza Nuova [New Power] and Lega Nord [the Northern League] – also opposes inclusive sexual health education programmes in schools, accusing them of manipulating children,[30] prematurely sexualising them and producing an extensively perverse society. The book of Genesis states (1:27) 'Male and Female God created them': for the Catholic Church, which gives a narrow rather than literal reading of this verse, the sexes must be two and no more than two, and have to be defined by their reciprocal attraction. Transgender, gay, lesbian and bisexual people are therefore banished from God's plan. And along with them are intersex people, although there can be no doubt about the 'naturalness' of their condition.

While the SIPSIS guide treats it as the exception that confirms the rule of the binary sex/gender system, the truth is that intersex is a reality that invalidates that same binary, demonstrating that, far from describing human nature, the binary actually coercively 'regulates' it, in some cases cruelly so. Intersex is indeed at the centre of the controversy against the so-called 'gender ideology', not only from a logical-conceptual perspective, but also from a historical one. Twenty years before the publication of the guide, in May 1995, the campaign against 'gender ideology' was in fact first announced on the Italian newspaper *la Repubblica* by an article revealingly titled: 'The Church Prepares for the War against the Five Sexes' (Politi, 1995).[31] The Pope at the time was Wojtyla, the UN was organising the World Conference on Women in Beijing, and a 29-page typescript had circulated in the preparatory forum of NGOs titled *Gender, the Deconstruction of Women*, which set off the angry reaction of the Vatican delegates and the Church's first public statements (Goetz and Baden, 1997). The author of the typescript was Dale O'Leary, a journalist of the conservative journal *Hearth – Journal of the Authentic Catholic Woman*. In it she complains against the use of the term 'gender' in the conference documents, presenting it as the forerunner of a proliferation of the sexes. Her attacks are mainly directed against philosopher Judith Butler's book *Gender Trouble: Feminism and the Subversion of Identity* (1990) – one of the founding texts of Queer Theory[32] as we shall soon see – and against biologist Anne Fausto-Sterling's article 'The Five Sexes: Why Male and Female are Not Enough' (1993), which is dedicated to the theme I will examine shortly, intersex. Before doing so, however, I will provide a short explanation of the condition itself.

As I mentioned in the first paragraph of this chapter, the term 'intersex'[33] refers to a multiplicity of physical conditions in which the six factors concerning biological sex previously mentioned (chromosomes, hormones, external and internal genitalia, secondary sex characteristics, gonads) are found in combinations considered atypical in relation to standard male and female attributes. The physical anatomies that can be associated with an intersex condition are numerous, especially if we bear in mind that standard male and female attributes are nothing but normative ideals, from which real bodies can easily diverge. Some of them are classified by contemporary medicine as 'syndromes' and designated through the acronym DSD, Disorders of Sex Development.[34] For the most part these designations are rejected by intersex movements – and I personally follow their rejection. However, I will make provisional use of them in order to briefly sketch out a few examples.

Forms of intersex representative of the atypical metabolism of testosterone in subjects with XY chromosomes are represented by the so-called Androgen Insensitivity Syndrome (AIS) and the steroid

5-alpha-reductase deficiency.[35] In both cases, the genitalia at birth are different from the standard ones. Even when they are completely similar to the vulva on the exterior, internally the vagina may be short, and in the abdomen there are testicles instead of the uterus and ovaries. In some cases of androgen insensitivity syndrome, and in almost all cases of steroid 5-alpha-reductase deficiency, a significant virilisation of the phenotype may occur in adolescence, including genitalia, with prominent growth of the erectile organ. According to medical statistics, most people with 5-alpha-reductase steroid deficiency have a male gender identity, while most people with androgen insensitivity syndrome have a female gender identity. Congenital Adrenal Hyperplasia is instead an intersexual condition related to the metabolism of testosterone in people with XX chromosomes, in which, due to a production of testosterone higher than the average for female bodies,[36] the clitoris may grow to the size of a penis, the vagina may be short and the vulva may be atypical. Furthermore, at onset of puberty the phenotype may evolve in the male direction. However, uterus and ovaries are present in this condition, and in most cases, according to statistics, the gender identity is female. Other physical constitutions that can be included in the intersex category are connected to the presence of atypical sex chromosomes. For example, people affected by the so-called Klinefelter syndrome have three sexual chromosomes, two Xs and a Y (XXY). Despite being born with male genitalia, they may not develop typically male secondary sex characteristics when they reach puberty. Their penis and testicles usually grow less than the average; they may develop breasts and large hips; libido may be absent or weak; and the beard may be absent or thin.

Another case of chromosomal variation is the genetic mosaic or mosaicism, wherein the body hosts two different sets of cells, some with XX chromosomes and others with XY chromosomes. People affected by mosaicism may have different traits: at birth they may have typically male genitalia, typically female genitalia, or intermediate genitalia. With puberty they can acquire both masculine and feminine traits (for example, they may have a female breast and at the same time a low voice and a beard). Their gonads may be comprised of mixed tissue, both ovarian and testicular (ovotestis), and may produce both sperm and eggs.

These are just some examples: there are plenty more intersex conditions.[37] They might be rare, but they have always been known in
all cultures. Because of the transgression they represent with respect
to the binary sex/gender system, in the past intersex people were
made sacred, thus both celebrated (see the myth of Hermaphroditus
and that of Tiresias) and persecuted (the sacred, as anthropology
teaches us, is both blessed and cursed by the gods). And their persecution did not end with the beginning of modern medicine. According to historian Alice Dreger (1998), two phases can be distinguished
in the mid-nineteenth century with regard to the history of modern
medicine's 'treatment' of intersex people. There is the 'gonads'
period, from 1870 to 1915 approximately, and the 'conversion'
period, which began soon after, and which could optimistically be
considered concluded in 2006, but in fact isn't. What the two periods
have in common is that, in both, medicine has been put to the service
of the binary sex/gender system and has studied the intersex condition mostly with the intention of erasing it, in order to confirm that
humanity is divided into males and females. The tactics used were,
however, different. During the 'gonads' period, an attempt was made
to turn intersex, which was then called hermaphroditism, into a very
rare condition, by trying to assign a true gender, male or female, to
most cases of atypical genitalia and phenotypes: what settled the
issue was, precisely, the presence of male or female gonads. It was
German pathologist Theodor Edwin Klebs (*Handbuch der pathologischen Anatomie*, 1868) who first introduced the distinction between
true hermaphroditism and male or female pseudo-hermaphroditism.
According to his definition, the former included only extremely rare
cases of intersex people with at least one testicle and one ovary (the
existence of gonads of mixed tissue had not yet been discovered),
whereas the latter included all the remaining intersex people that had
to be recognised as either male or female, albeit 'abnormal'.[38] In the
absence of ultrasound technology, however, the internal gonads
could not be observed except by exploratory surgery, which was
performed very rarely, or after death, in autopsies. Since the possibility of true hermaphroditism was discarded *a priori*, someone's
'real sex' was assigned then by interpreting as signs of the presence of
testicles or ovaries either the appearance of the genitals and of secondary sex characteristics, or – and this what interests us here the
most – the direction of sexual desire.

An enlightening example is Herculine Barbin, nicknamed Alexina, born in Saint-Jean-d'Angély in 1838, whose memoirs were published by Foucault in 1978 (see Foucault, 1980), along with the autopsy reports. From these we know that as an adult Alexina had a face covered with downy hairs, and a body without female breasts, uterus and ovaries, with a hint of a vagina, a 'hypertrophic' clitoris or a 'small' penis, two skin folds that could be interpreted as a vulva's major labia or as lobes of a divided scrotum – one of which contained a testicle, while the other testicle was located inside the abdomen. The shape of her external genitalia was certainly visible at birth, and yet, because of the presence of a hint of vagina, and because of the small size of her penis, she was assigned to the female sex and was educated as a girl. The problems began in 1860, when, while teaching in a boarding school for girls, she fell in love, reciprocated, with her colleague Sara – and had the terrible idea of confessing her feelings and all her personal history to the bishop of La Rochelle, who, with her consent, had her examined by a doctor. The opinion of Dr Chesnet and a judgment of the court of Saint-Jean-d'Angély eventually ratified the change of gender on her birth certificate from woman to man, establishing that the doctors who had visited her as a newborn had made a mistake. Herculine became Abel and was forced to wear men's clothes and quit her job. She/he began a wandering life, which ended badly. In 1868, at the age of thirty, she committed suicide with the fumes of a coal stove, leaving a letter in which she claimed to have taken her own life in order to escape suffering. This tragic story is exemplary for understanding the functioning of that fundamental norm of the sex/gender binary, which in an enlightening essay published in 1980 Adrienne Rich (1980) called 'compulsory heterosexuality'. According to this norm, it is not only impossible to think anything beyond just two sexes/genders, but these latter are *defined exclusively by their mutual attraction*. It is by virtue of this norm that the religious, medical and legal authorities had no doubt, *after* her confession, as to the sex Alexina should be assigned to, even though they were in the presence of an indiscernible anatomy. In the regime of compulsory heterosexuality, where only heterosexual desire is conceivable, the fact that Alexina liked women, and that women liked Alexina, meant that she could only be a man.[39]

Far from waning off with the end of the 'gonads' period, the norms of the sex/gender binary and of compulsory heterosexuality continued to prescribe the erasure of the intersex condition even in the period of 'conversion', and this time they did so literally. Indeed, after the first decade of the twentieth century – and with increasing efficacy after the 1950s – when it came to intersex cases, medicine did not limit itself to ascertaining the person's 'real sex' by interpreting signs on the patient's body, but it fully produced it by intervening on their body with plastic surgery and hormonal therapies. The manifesto of this new medical trend can be found in the so-called Hopkins protocols (Money et al., 1955), developed by the research team of the Gender Identity Clinics of the Johns Hopkins Hospital in Baltimore, directed by psychologist John Money – that is, by the same Money who authored, together with John and Joan Hampson, the already mentioned 1957 article which sanctioned the difference between sex and gender.[40] These psychologists were convinced that every infant, of any sex, was born sexually neutral (or bisexual, in the Freudian sense, that is, susceptible of psychological development either towards the male or female spectrum), and that gender identity depended exclusively on the education received in one's first three years of life. They also believed that among the factors listed above, the decisive social and psychological one for determining one's own belonging to one of the two sexes was the structure of the genitalia, considered not only from the aesthetic point of view, but also according to the parameter of functionality with reference to heterosexual coitus (penis-vagina penetration). According to these two principles, the Hopkins protocols required that intersex infants undergo as soon as possible plastic genital surgery and hormonal therapies that would make their bodies as similar as possible to standard male or female ones (i.e. that would 'convert' them into females or males). The protocols also required that intersex children be raised in rigid conformity to their assigned gender, keeping them ignorant of their own condition.[41] The Hopkins protocols were improved at the end of the 1980s by a team lead by Patricia Donahoe (Donahoe, 1987; Donahoe et al., 1991), director of the Paediatric Surgical Research Laboratories at the Massachusetts General Hospital. She established that in order for the penis to be able to penetrate a woman's vagina, it shouldn't measure less than 2.5 cm at birth; and that in order for the clitoris not to be able to penetrate any sexual orifice, it shouldn't be longer than 0.9 cm at birth. According to these criteria, for decades the so-called 'hypertrophy' of the clitoris was 'corrected' in infants, with the risk of depriving them of orgasmic sensitivity. Moreover, their vaginas were deepened when they were considered too short to be penetrated by a penis. In addition, due to the difficulty of performing phalloplasty surgeries, for a long time most intersex infants were designated female. It is worth repeating that this is all due to that dispositive of power which is modern sexuality, according to which only two sexes/genders are possible (the binary sex/gender system) and they are understood only through their complementarity, defined in terms of heterosexual desire during the 'gonads' period, and in terms of heterosexual coitus during the 'conversion' period (compulsory heterosexuality).

It was to respond to this dramatic situation that in 1993, two years before the UN conference in Beijing, Fausto-Sterling – now Professor Emeritus at Brown University – wrote the article 'The Five Sexes: Why Male and Female Are Not Enough', where she reinterpreted in a non-pathological key Klebs's old distinction between true hermaphrodites and pseudohermaphrodites, by way of electing not only the gonads (as in Klebs's model) but also the conformation of the genitalia (as in Money's model) as distinctive criteria. Challenging the sex/gender binary's underlying common sense, Fausto-Sterling argued that medicine should recognise the existence of at least five sexes: in addition to females and males, Fausto-Sterling (1993, p.21) proposed the 'ferms', once called female pseudohermaphrodites ('who have ovaries and some aspects of the male genitalia, but lack testes'), the 'herms', once called true hermaphrodites ('who possess one testis and one ovary'), and the 'merms', once called male pseudohermaphrodites ('who have testes and some aspects of the female genitalia but no ovaries'). These are indeed the five sexes that set off alarm bells for O'Leary and the Vatican delegates at the 1995 Women's Conference in Beijing.

It is true that Fausto-Sterling's (1993) proposal clashes with the binary and heterosexist anthropology defended by the Catholic Church. However, we must understand that, contrary to what is proclaimed in the anti-gender campaign, recognising the existence of at least five sexes does not mean hypothesising the sexual neutrality of children and promoting the manipulation of their identities. Actually, this is exactly what medicine has been proposing for a long time in the wake of Money and Donahoe's theories, not to mention their predecessors. Recognising the existence of at least five sexes is, on the contrary, a way to oppose the manipulation of the sex of children, and in particular to resist the surgical violence exerted on intersex children in the name of the sex/gender binary and compulsory heterosexuality. It is not a question of spreading an ideology bent on 'producing' five sexes ... the five sexes are already there! And even more than five, actually, if we care to look carefully enough.

'The Five Sexes' was published in the prestigious journal *The Sciences*, accompanied by a few brief commentaries, the first of which, titled 'Intersexual Rights', was written by Cheryl Chase, who had founded the ISNA (Intersex Society of North America) in San Francisco in 1993. Cheryl Chase is the pseudonym of Bonnie Sullivan, born Brian Sullivan in 1956, and who changed her name to Bo Laurent in 1995. Cheryl was an intersex person with XX chromosomes who was raised male until she was eighteen months old, when she was assigned to the female gender, after an operation in which her erectile organ was removed, and which was followed seven years later by the removal of the testicular part of her ovotestes (Baird, 2001, p.117). Her commentary on Fausto-Sterling's article was a condemnation of the multiple traumas that surgeries and ceaseless medical examinations, such as those she underwent, leave on the body and mind of intersex people:

Many 'graduates' of medical intersex corrective programs are chronically depressed, wishing vainly for the return of body parts. Suicides are not uncommon. Some former intersexuals become transsexuals, rejecting their imposed sex. Follow-up studies of adults to ascertain the long-term outcome of intervention are conspicuously absent ... Medical dogma of sex assignment of intersexuals centres on the 'adequacy' of the penis. Because a large penis cannot be constructed from a small one, female assignment is preferred. Because a large clitoris is considered 'disfiguring', extensive surgery is employed to remove, trim or relocate it. Whereas a male with an 'inadequate' penis (small but with normal erotic sensation) is considered tragic, the same person transformed into a female with reduced or absent genital sensation and an artificial vagina is considered normal. The capacity to inflict such monstrous 'treatment' on children who cannot consent, is ultimately a clear expression of the hatred and fear of sexuality that predominate in our culture.

(Chase, 1993, p.3)

Chase's piece ended with the announcement that the ISNA was organising a support group and was collecting information material on the lives of intersex people, and with an invitation for them to contact the association. The invitation did not remain unheeded, and three years later, on 26 October 1996, the ISNA managed to organise its first public demonstration against the genital mutilation of intersex children in front of the Hynes Auditorium in Boston, where the annual meeting of the American Association of Paediatrics was being held. Chase's text also started a dialogue and a negotiation with the scientific community thanks to which, in 2006, the two most influential associations of paediatric endocrinology in the world, the Lawson Wilkins Pediatric Endocrine Society and the European Society for Paediatric Endocrinology, published an official document, the 'Consensus Statement on Management of Intersex Disorders' (Hughes et al., 2006), in which they condemned the Hopkins protocols and defended the principle of informed consent. According to this principle, intersex people should be made aware of their situation and should not undergo plastic surgery unless expressly requested by the subjects themselves. In the following years, the ISNA couldn't help but happily register the increasing attention given by the medical-psychological community to the intersex question. And in 2008 it ceased its activities.

It would be, however, too optimistic to believe that the 'conversion' period definitely ended in 2006, and that the intersex question is now resolved. It is true that in 2014 the UN and the WHO declared plastic surgery on healthy genitalia without the consent of the person concerned a violation of human rights. Currently however, only Colombia (since 1999, following a Constitutional Court's verdict) and Malta (since 2015, by law) have explicitly prohibited these surgeries, whereas Germany adopted a controversial rule in 2013, which allows the non-assignment of sex at birth to an intersex infant. Moreover, there are still no accurate statistics on the medical treatment of intersex people,[42] and numerous testimonies enable us to ascertain that the barbarity of non-consensual genital surgery on intersex children is far from over. In Italy, for example, a decision of the 2010 National Committee for Bioethics confirms the principle of informed consent, but also that

> medical and surgical interventions on the body ... are not only legitimate, but also required if they represent the only reasonable and practicable way to ensure – as far as possible – that the person enjoys the conditions for achieving a harmonious identification in the future, including also the possibility of having an active sex life.[43]
>
> (Presidenza del Consiglio dei Ministri, Comitato Nazionale per la Bioetica, 2010, p.16)

Furthermore, in a brochure distributed in 2014 at the San Raffaele Hospital in Milan, parents of girls with Congenital Adrenal Hyperplasia are advised to have doctors intervene on their daughter's clitoris and vagina within the first year of their child's life, in order to 'correct the anatomical alteration (aesthetic aspect) and allow their daughters to have normal and satisfactory sexual relations as adults (functional aspect)' (Russo et al., 2014).[44] In Italy, as in many other parts of the world, the sex/gender binary and compulsory heterosexuality are therefore far from having lost their normative hold on the life of intersex people. The results obtained by the intersex movements were important, but not sufficient, to end the 'conversion' period and the harmful consequences of the over-medicalisation of intersex people. Proof of this is also the fact that the 'Consensus Statement' is the document that introduced the contested wording 'Disorders of Sex Development'. For these reasons, after the dissolution of the ISNA, other groups took over, including, at global level, the OII, Organisation Internationale des Intersexués [International Intersex Organisation] (founded by Curtis Hinkle in 2003 with the aim of promoting the visibility of intersex people also outside the United States and English-speaking countries). In Italy the collective Intersexioni has been active since 2013 and in its political programme the defence of intersex rights intersects with other struggles, such those for LGBT rights, and feminist, antiracist and antispecist struggles.[45]

Already in 2000, following the flourishing of intersex activism, Fausto-Sterling felt compelled to publish a second article on the

journal *The Sciences*, which opens with a tribute to Cheryl Chase
and to ISNA, continues with a clear condemnation of the Hopkins
protocols and of genital mutilations performed on children, and
ends with a revision of her own theory of the five sexes. The
essay's title is 'The Five Sexes Revisited' (Fausto-Sterling, 2000),[46]
and it constitutes – among other things – also a response to the
Catholic Church's campaign, which had begun with the UN conference in Beijing. Faced with controversy, instead of backing off,
Fausto-Sterling (2000) on the one hand declares all her pride for
having contributed with her first article to the consolidation of the
intersex movement;[47] on the other hand, she also raises the stakes.
Her thesis is now that the model of the five sexes is insufficient to
give an account of intersexuality because it is still linked to an
obsolete medical idea that makes genitalia and gonads prevail over
all other factors in the determination of sex and gender (and, as
mentioned above, there are at least ten of such factors). Taking
into account the complexity of human sexuality, Fausto-Sterling
suggests that instead of placing the sexes along a continuous
straight line that has male and female at its extremes, it would be
better to conceptualise sex and gender as a range of points in a
multidimensional space:

> It might seem natural to regard intersexuals and transgendered
> people as living midway between the poles of male and female.
> But male and female, masculine and feminine, cannot be parsed
> as some kind of continuum. Rather, sex and gender are best
> conceptualized as points in a multidimensional space. For some
> time, experts on gender development have distinguished
> between sex at the genetic level and at the cellular level (sex-
> specific gene expression, X and Y chromosomes); at the hor-
> monal level (in the fetus, during childhood and after puberty);
> and at the anatomical level (genitals and secondary sexual
> characteristics). Gender identity presumably emerges from all
> of those corporeal aspects via some poorly understood interac-
> tion with environment and experience. What has become
> increasingly clear is that one can find levels of masculinity and
> femininity in almost every possible permutation.
>
> (2000, p.22)

As it should be clear at this point, it can happen for example that a person who is male from a chromosomal and hormonal point of view, might not metabolise testosterone and have atypical genitalia, which are externally female, and have female gender identity; or it can happen that a person with female chromosomes, high foetal production of male hormones, masculine genitalia and production of female hormones in puberty, has a female gender identity. The possible combinations are many, even at the level of identity. A transgender woman, for example, can have a penis without this putting into question her female identity, and she can be a lesbian and have active penetrative sex with her female partner. All this does not need to be planned by an ideology: it already happens all around us; we just need to observe reality without the actual ideological filters of the sex/gender binary and of compulsory heterosexuality.

Analysing how contemporary sexuality works from the point of view of transgender and intersex people allows us therefore to understand immediately what Foucault means when he claims that sexuality is a dispositive of power that can be resisted. The pressure of the sex-gender-sexual orientation classification system upon intersex and transgender bodies during the twentieth century took on such scope of surgical and juridical violence that made it all the more clearly observable. At the same time, the struggles and achievements of intersex and transgender movements are a clear demonstration of the historical, arbitrary and mutable nature of this classification system, which can be challenged and modified not only by intersex and transgender subjects themselves, but by all those who feel oppressed by the binary sex/gender system and by compulsory heterosexuality. Many of the contradictions that have first emerged in the analysis of the concept of 'sexual orientation' arise, for example, from the fact that in the modern imaginary male and female genders are already defined by heterosexuality, which actually renders paradoxical the identities of male and female homosexuals. Again, gay and lesbian movements and gay and lesbian communities have not only been able to claim and gain rights, but also gain visibility and recognition, to the point that – as I have already stated – it is now possible to argue that a new social imaginary has emerged in which 'gay' and 'lesbian' have acquired the status of genders, beside those of male and female heterosexuals, transgender people, etc.

The proposal Fausto-Sterling arrived at, however, makes it clear that challenging the sex/gender binary and compulsory heterosexuality does not necessarily mean that gender differences must be definitively abolished for everyone, in the name of a presumed 'truth' or 'naturalness' of sex that would bypass the male-female polarity. In the perspective opened by her second article, in fact, this polarity, far from being erased, is multiplied by a process of diffraction that projects it on different levels. Queer theories are indeed divided with regards to the possibility of definitively overthrowing the power that governs sexuality. A first, simplifying way to articulate the distinction between revolutionary Freudo-Marxism and radical constructivism would be to notice that for the former it is possible to bring out the truth of human sexuality, which has been repressed by power, whereas for the latter such truth does not exist, or rather it exists only insofar as it is produced by power itself. As for anti-social queer theories, we could argue – again drastically simplifying the matter – that they are opposed to radical constructivism, insofar as they view it as responsible of an excessive politicisation – and thus 'desexualisation' – of sex. As I have mentioned before, the three theoretical approaches also differ with respect to which dimension of sexuality, among many, they favour as the vantage point for their observations. This chapter's critical exercise in an ontology of actuality has already clarified how radical constructivism analyses sexuality above all as an *identity-producing* historical dispositive of power and has illustrated *how* it works. The next chapter will also show *what* sexuality is for revolutionary Freudo-Marxism and for antisocial theories: that is, primarily *desire* for the former, and essentially *drive* for the latter.

Notes

1 I will briefly discuss the no-gender campaign at the beginning of the next paragraph. On the topic see Garbagnoli (2014) '"L'ideologia del genere". L'irresistibile ascesa di un'invenzione retorica vaticana contro la denaturalizzazione dell'ordine sessuale'. I also suggest Bernini (2014) 'Uno spettro si aggira per l'Europa... Sugli usi e gli abusi del concetto di "gender"', and (2016) 'La "teoria del gender", i "negazionisti" e la "fine della differenza sessuale"'. Translators' note: The Italian terms used for 'gender ideology' are 'teoria del gender' and 'ideologia del gender', respectively 'gender theory' and 'gender ideology'. As it is

evident from the Italian expression, the noun 'gender' is an English loan-word, its pointed non-translation serving to underscore the foreignness of the concept itself, as if 'gender' is something other, which supposedly does not belong to Italian culture.

2 The book is downloadable for free from the association's website (at the following address: www.sipsis.it/il-genere-una-guida-orientativa/) and is supported by the Fondazione Genere Identità e Cultura [Gender Identity and Culture Foundation] (GIC), by the Centro di Ateneo Sinapsi of the University of Naples 'Federico II', and by the Osservatorio Nazionale sull'Identità di Genere [National Observatory on Gender Identity] (ONIG). These are progressive institutions like SIPSIS itself.

3 In the second section of this chapter (the next one) I will clarify the meaning of the term 'transgender', whereas I will talk about the intersex condition in the third section.

4 The definition of 'phenotype' will be given shortly. There has been extensive debate on the influence of hormones on the brain structure. The SIPSIS guide considers this debate as settled. Ferrari et al. (2015) explain: 'The study of the structure and functioning of the brain of males and females has shown, in some cases, some differences in the "hemispheric lateralisation" – the fact that the two hemispheres specialise in different functions – which is considered more prominent in males and less prominent in females. More recent studies have found, instead, differences in the response of some specific areas of the brain, such as the amygdala, a structure involved in the analysis of emotions. The response of the left amygdala to negative emotional stimuli seems to be more intense in females, while males seem to respond more intensely to positive emotional stimuli. However, extensive and in-depth meta-analysis of the thousands of studies on the subject, proved these results wrong, and showed that the publications that supported them did not take into account the social factors that contribute to the development of the brain. It needs to be noted that the structures and functions of the brain are "plastic", that is, they also change on the basis of life experiences and learning, and the results found are sometimes compatible with the effects of gender socialisation' (p.24). However, it is not uncommon to find the thesis that female and male brains are biologically different being re-hashed by experts, or self-styled ones.

5 In the fourth edition of the *DSM* (the *Diagnostic and Statistical Manual of Mental Disorders*, published by the American Psychiatric Association, which I will discuss extensively in the next paragraph) asexuality was conflated with HSDD (Hypoactive Sexual Desire Disorder). However, the supporting text to the fifth edition of the *DSM*, published in 2013, states that people who define themselves as asexual should not be diagnosed with this disorder. This change of perspective was achieved thanks to the commitment of asexual activists who within approximately a decade have managed to engage in a fruitful conversation with

the psychiatry community. In 2001, in the United States, David Jay founded AVEN (Asexual Visibility & Education Network), from which the AVEN DSM taskforce emerged. The online platform also inspired the formation of an Italian asexual community (www.asexuality.org.it), AVEN Italia, founded in 2005. The website of the community, www.asessuali.com, was added in 2011.

6 Translators' note: 'binary sex/gender system' translates Bernini's expression 'binarismo sessuale', which can also be translated as 'gender binary'. As we noted in Chapter 1 (note 21), 'sesso' and 'sessuale' in Italian can mean both (biological) 'sex' and (socially constructed) 'gender'. However, since Bernini in this chapter focuses on intersex activism and explores the complexities of biological 'sex', we opted to use the expression 'sex/gender binary'. In this first iteration, we further added the word 'system' ('sex/gender binary *system*') to clarify that we are not referring to the binary divide *between* sex and gender (wherein sex is an exclusively biological fact and gender an exclusively social one), but to the idea that *both* sex *and* gender are constructed as binary (male/female, man/woman). This clarification is particularly important in the context of Bernini's argument, particularly since over the last two decades transgender movements have strongly critiqued rigid feminist understandings of the divide *between* sex and gender, as these frequently have the effect of excluding transwomen from women-only spaces (feminist thinkers who support such exclusions are identified as 'trans exclusionary feminists', or 'terfs'). This said, from this point in the text onward, the reader will encounter the abbreviated expressions 'sex/gender binary' and 'binary system'. In both instances the reader should note that we are still translating Bernini's Italian expression 'binarismo sessuale'.

7 'Biopolitics' is the concept introduced by Foucault (1976) in the last chapter of *La volonté de savoir*, to indicate the processes of governance of the life of populations developed in conjunction with the birth of the modern state. I will return to the concept in Chapter 3.

8 The term 'transvestite', still used in psychiatry, is being currently criticised by transgender communities because it is considered derogatory and misleading. In these same communities – as I will repeat shortly – the term 'transgender' is now preferred to the term 'transsexual', the former understood as an indicator of a wide range of identities, including those once called 'transsexual'. See: World Professional Association for Transgender Health, WPATH ICD-11 *Consensus Meeting*, 31 May 2013.

9 On the genesis of the concept of 'gender', its evolution in the work by Money, its reception in subsequent medical-psychological studies and the criticism of the binary sex/gender system in the most recent developments of biology, see Busi (2016).

10 It is important to note that the terms used by sexologists, first in Germany and then internationally, to indicate sexual minorities were

coined by the first activists belonging to these minorities themselves. In other words, those directly impacted by these designations were not passive objects of psychological studies, but subjects who actively contributed to the construction and acknowledgement of their identities. The terms 'homosexuality' and 'heterosexuality' first appeared in an essay that in 1869 the Hungarian intellectual Karl Maria Kertbeny sent to the Prussian government to protest against the addition of the paragraph against sodomy in the Prussian penal code to the penal code of the new Confederation of Northern Germany. This is narrated by Havelock Ellis in *Sexual Inversion*, who found the information in a letter in which Karl Heinrich Ulrichs claimed that Kertbeny had coined the term 'homosexuality' because he was envious of the fortune of the term 'uranism', which Ulrichs himself had invented (drawing from the goddess Aphrodite Urania, who in Plato's *Symposium* is invoked as the protector of love between men). Magnus Hirschfeld coined, on the other hand, both the term 'transvestite' (in his 1910 book *Die Transvestiten*) and the term 'transsexuality' (the expression 'seelischer Transexualismus', transsexuality of the soul, is found in his 1923 article 'Die intersexuelle Konstitution'). However, for Hirschfeld, there was continuity between the terms uranism, transvestism and transsexuality, as they were understood as nuances of what he called the 'third sex' or 'intermediate sexual condition', following the inversion model. With the term 'homosexuality', Kertbeny wanted instead to reclaim the 'manhood' of men who are sexually attracted to other men, their full identification with the male gender (thus anticipating the current concept of homosexual orientation), against the inversion model that Ulrichs as well had adopted. On the contribution of early homosexual activism to the emergence of the notion of homosexual identity and to the interpretative model of inversion, and in particular on the fundamental role played by Ulrichs and Hirschfeld, see Beachy (2014).

11 Translators' note: the law of 20 May 2016, n. 76, art 1, comma 1 states that: 'The present law establishes the civil union between same sex couples as specific social formation'. This means that same-sex couples do not constitute a family, but a specific social formation. This is confirmed by the fact that the law does not contemplate the fidelity obligation and neither the stepchild adoption, that is, the possibility to adopt the child of the partner, which instead are, respectively, an obligation and a right contemplated by the marriage law. This means that same-sex couples are de facto excluded from the same rights and obligations enjoyed by heterosexual couples.

12 In 1974 the so-called 'egosyntonic homosexuality' (subjects who accept their homosexual desire and harmoniously integrate it within their personality) was removed from the list, and the same happened in 1987 for 'egodystonic homosexuality' (subjects who live their homosexual desire with discomfort). Finally, on 17 May 1990, the World Health Organization removed homosexuality from the International Classification of

Diseases (ICD). It is because of this that the World Day against Homophobia is celebrated on 17 May each year.

13 The category of 'transsexualism' had been added to the ICD (see previous note) five years earlier, in 1975.

14 Also in this case, the name had appeared in the ICD (see previous notes) earlier, in 1990.

15 Christin Jorgensen was operated on in Denmark in 1951 by Dr Christian Hamburger (her chosen name was in homage to him). Twenty years earlier, in 1930, in Berlin, Lili Elbe (born as Einar Wegener) underwent, under the supervision of Magnus Hirschfeld, the first of a series of experimental surgeries, which led to her death within a year.

16 Vaginoplasty and phalloplasty are invasive and complex operations, which can lead to serious complications. To this day, phalloplasty can cause strong rejection. The most frequent risks associated with vaginoplasty are stenosis of the new vagina and loss of orgasmic capacity. The progress of surgical techniques and post-operative therapies is making these risks less and less frequent but has not yet succeeded in eliminating them altogether.

17 See also Marcasciano (2002, 2008, 2014).

18 'On a sunny and hot day in the summer of 1979, in a crowded public swimming pool in Milan, a group of transsexuals staged a singular and striking protest. Given that they were not recognised by the institutions as transsexuals, least of all as women, they decided to wear male swimsuits, which meant that their breasts were exposed, thus demonstrating their real gender affiliation. The protest spread in all the Italian cities where transsexual communities were present. Its main objectives were the recognition of one's identity and the approval of a law for sex change and consequent change of name on documents' (Marcasciano, 2006, p.42).

19 In the United States, at the University of Arizona, Susan Stryker has recently inaugurated a specialised honours degree in Transgender Studies. Susan Stryker is also the editor (first with Stephen Whittle and then with Aren Z. Aizura) of two volumes of *The Transgender Studies Reader* (2006 and 2013). For Stryker's work on the history of the transgender movement in the United States see (2008) 'Transgender History, Homonormativity and Disciplinarity', translated in Italian by Adriano J. Habed (Stryker, 2015) 'Una storia del movimento transgender: esperienza, omonormatività e pratiche disciplinari'.

20 In *Transgender Warriors* (1996) Feinberg wrote: 'the term *transgenderist* was first introduced into the English language by trans warrior Virginia Prince. Virginia told me, "I coined the noun transgenderist in 1987 or '88. There had to be some name for people like myself who trans the gender barrier – meaning somebody who lives full time in the gender opposite to their anatomy. I have not transed the sex barrier"' (p.X). As the overall transgender movement continues to develop, more people are exploring the distinction between a person's sex – female, intersex,

male – and their gender expression – feminine, androgynous, masculine and other variations. Many national and local gender magazines and community groups are starting to use 'TS/TG: transsexual and transgender'. Twenty years later, within activist circles the term 'transgender' is increasingly used to indicate both transgender people in the strict sense of the term, and those once called 'transsexuals' or 'transvestites'. According to Stryker: 'Robert Hill, who has been researching the history of heterosexual male cross-dressing communities, found instances in community-based publications of words like *transgenderal*, *transgenderist*, and *transgenderism* dating back to the late 1960s. The logic of those terms, used to describe individuals who lived in one social gender but had a bodily sex conventionally associated with the other, aimed for a conceptual middle ground between transvestism (merely changing one's clothing) and transsexualism (changing one's sex). By the early 1990s, primarily through the influence of Leslie Feinberg's 1992 pamphlet *Transgender Liberation: A Movement Whose Time Has Come*, *transgender* was beginning to refer to something else – an imagined political alliance of all possible forms of gender antinormativity. It was in this latter sense that *transgender* became articulated with *queer*' (2008, p.146).

21 See Feinberg (1993), *Stone Butch Blues*, a novel partially inspired by Feinberg's own life experiences.

22 The repetition of 'read' in this passage is ironic: the verb is used first in a literal sense ('to the brothers and sisters who may read the text that I have written'), and is subsequently signalled with inverted commas to indicate the act of deciphering transgenderism ('to the brothers and sisters who read me, that is, who recognise, underneath my feminine appearance, that the sex assigned to me at birth was male').

23 On the legal status of transgender people in Italy until 2013 see Lorenzetti (2013).

24 To give some examples, Germany has been authorising the so-called 'small solution' (kleine lösung) since the 1980s (i.e. the change of name in the documents without the need for surgery or hormonal treatment). In Argentina since 2012, in Denmark since 2014 and in Malta and Ireland since 2015, it is possible to change the name on documents with a simple self-certification, without the need for surgery, sterilisation or medical-psychiatric reports.

25 To learn more about the debate around depathologisation within Italian transgender movements, see Arietti et al. (2010). The SIPSIS guide's approach to this issue is, to say the least, ambivalent. On the one hand it argues that transgender people should not be considered sick. However, on the other hand it complains that the Italian law does not include the *obligation* for psychological support: 'The fact that the Italian law does not envisage compulsory psychological support to be included in the process may be in certain cases a problem: not because, as we have said, transgender people are psychologically ill, but because

it can be risky to start such a delicate and irreversible path without an adequate network of support, as this might pose a threat to the psychological and physical health of transgender people. It takes a lot of strength, endurance and resilience to face the lengthy process of transition, and that's why psychological support might be required, even though it may sometimes be refused for fear of being unduly pathologised' (Ferrari et al., 2015, pp.54–55).

26 The Pope had similarly intervened against the term 'gender' already four years prior, in his 'Discorso del Santo Padre Benedetto XVI alla Curia romana per la presentazione degli auguri natalizi' (Ratzinger, 2008).

27 For example, Pope Bergoglio defined 'gender ideology' as 'a mistake of the human mind that creates a lot of confusion' (Scaramuzzi, 2015) and as 'the outcome of a frustration and a resignation that aims to erase sexual difference because it can no longer deal with it' (Bergoglio, 2015). Moreover, while the Italian Senate was preparing to discuss the bill on civil unions for same-sex couples in January 2016, he stated that homosexual people 'live in an objective state of error' and that 'there can be no confusion between the divinely ordained family and other kinds of union' (Bergoglio, 2016).

28 In 2012, and before then in 2008 (see note 26 above), Ratzinger challenged the use of the term 'gender' itself. Paragraph 58 of the Relatio Finalis of the Synod on the Family, approved in October 2015, argues, instead, that 'soul and body, as well as biological sex and the social-cultural role of sex (gender), can be distinguished, but not separated'. The Synod has thus agreed to the use of the term 'gender', provided that it refers only to the male and the female genders, understood as the socio-cultural expression of the male sex in the former case, and of the female sex in the latter.

29 Because of the reactionary no-gender protests, the controversial bill against inciting hatred towards homosexual people, which was approved in September 2013 by the Chamber of Deputies, has never been discussed by the Senate. In addition, in March 2014, the Ministry of Education, University and Research of the Renzi government blocked the dissemination of leaflets on diversity education in schools, which, according to a project approved by the previous Monti government, should have been distributed to Italian teachers. Finally, the civil unions law for lesbian and gay couples, which was passed in the Senate in February 2016, affirms the same principle of exclusion declared by Bergoglio, according to which a same-sex couple is not a family (see note 27 above).

30 In April 2014, for example, Bergoglio warns against 'the horrors of educational manipulation', which risk turning schools into 're-education camps' comparable to those of the 'great genocidal dictatorships of the 20th century' (2014).

31 Judith Butler comments on this article in 'The End of Sexual Difference' (2004).

32 Translators' note: 'Queer Theory' here translates the Italian phrase 'teorie queer propriamente dette' ('properly named queer theories'). In Chapter 3 Bernini further delineates a specific genealogical trajectory for queer theories, which he differentiates from these 'properly named queer theories'. In short, 'teorie queer propriamente dette' in Bernini's book, is a phrase that refers to the collection of primarily North American publications in English by authors such as Butler and Sedgwick (among many others), which between the 1990s and 2000s came to form the canonical backbone of academic research in the field of Queer Theory (wherein capitalisation and the use of 'Theory' as a collective noun signal the institutional sedimentation of such research). We have thus decided to translate with 'Queer Theory' whenever Bernini refers to such body of work (primarily coming from the United States and primarily published between the 1990s and the 2000s) in contrast to the specific genealogy of queer theories (in the plural and in small caps) that Bernini himself is offering in the book. See Chapter 3, note 15 (translators' note).

33 The term was coined by biologist Richard Goldschmidt, not with reference to human beings but to butterflies, in the article 'Intersexuality and the Endocrine Aspect of Sex' (1917).

34 The acronym was introduced in Hughes et al. (2006).

35 The steroid 5-alpha-reductase is the enzyme in charge of the conversion of testosterone to dihydrotestosterone, which is more akin to androgen receptors and therefore more 'potent' than testosterone.

36 This 'syndrome' concerns either people with chromosomes XY or people with chromosomes XX. In both cases, the increase in testosterone production is caused by the atypical functioning of the adrenal glands that produce less cortisol and aldosterone than average. In the syndrome's 'salt-losing' form, the total lack of production of the two hormones causes also serious problems in the sodium intake and in the excretion of potassium. If this syndrome is not promptly recognised and treated, it can lead to the newborn's death mere weeks after birth.

37 For further reading on the topic in Italian, see Crocetti (2013).

38 Or simply 'ugly'. See Pasotti (2017).

39 Revealingly, the three authorities did not question the nature of Sara's desires.

40 See note 9 above.

41 A paradigmatic example of the violence perpetrated in the name of the Hopkins protocols is the infamous story of David Reimer, born Bruce Reimer in 1965. As a newborn his body conformed to male standards, but during a circumcision surgery, his penis was accidentally amputated. After having seen an interview with Money on television, his parents made an appointment with him at the Gender Identity Clinic, where they were persuaded to turn Bruce into a female, whom they named 'Brenda'. When Brenda was twenty-two months old his testicles were amputated, and a rudimentary vulva was modelled on his body.

He was also subjected to a feminising hormone treatment, rigidly educated as a girl and kept in the dark about his personal story. Money
presented the case in a series of academic publications as proof of the
success of his theories. Brenda, however, never adapted to a female
identity. In his teens, he indeed openly rebelled against his parents and
refused to undergo any more of Money's annual examinations, threatening to commit suicide. At the age of fourteen, he finally managed to
get his parents to tell him the truth, and he decided to take on his original male identity, choosing to name himself 'David'. He began a new
therapy with surgical procedures (mastoplasty, phalloplasty) and mas-
culinising hormone therapy. Sexologist Milton Diamond (1997) and
journalist John Colapinto (2000) collected and publicly told his story,
exposing Money's intellectual dishonesty. David committed suicide in
2004, at the age of thirty-eight.

42 An exception is represented by an Australian study by Jones et al.
(2015). With regards to Italy, Michela Balocchi has been carrying out
research funded by the European Research Council, whose results have
been recently published (see Balocchi, 2019).

43 The document states that 'exceptionally, in some more difficult cases (i.e.
cases where there might be no objective data on which to base a sex
assignment's decision), it may not be appropriate to resort immediately to
removal and/or reconstructive surgeries because they may not be compatible with the actual development of sexual identity', but recommends that
in any case 'education is oriented according to the principles of gender
binarism, and thus either in a masculine or feminine way, paying great
attention to the observation of the child's genuine inclinations and to the
gradual emergence of its sexual awareness' (Presidenza del Consiglio dei
Ministri, Comitato Nazionale per la Bioetica, 2010, p.17).

44 The brochure is sponsored by SIP (Società Italian Pediatria [Italian Paediatric Society]), SIPPS (Società Italiana Pediatria Preventiva e Sociale
[Italian Society of Preventive and Social Paediatrics]), SIEDP (Società
Italiana Endocrinologia e Diabetologia Pediatrica [Italian Society of
Endocrinology and Pediatric Diabetology]), SIMA (Società Italiana Med-
icina dell'Adolescenza [Italian Society of Adolescent Medicine]). The
authors state that 'it is necessary … to intervene surgically to reduce the
excessive size of the clitoris and to correct the appearance of the vagina
by separating the aperture of the urinary tract from the opening of the
vagina. Generally, the surgical procedure is performed early, in the first
year of life, to prevent the child from being psychologically disturbed by
the modification of her genitalia. Most of the time the surgery is done all
at once, with a potential "revision" during puberty'.

45 On the various forms of activism by intersex people and by groups of
patients with DSDs in Italy, see Arfini and Crocetti (2015).

46 Fausto-Sterling (2000, p.22) argues that the criticism she received by
psychologist Suzanne Kessler (1998) made her reconsider her positions.
According to Kessler, in her first article Fausto-Sterling had given

genitalia the primacy of determining a person's gender, without taking into account the fact that in everyday life gender attributions do not operate through genital inspections. The two texts by Fausto-Sterling and Chase's commentary are published in Italian in an anthology of texts on intersex issues edited by Michela Balocchi (2019) for the book series *àltera – Politiche e teorie della sessualità* [*Politics and theories of sexuality*] by ETS Editions.

47 Fausto-Sterling (2000) states: 'No one could have foreseen such changes in 1993. And the idea that I played some role, however small, in reducing the pressure – from the medical community as well as from society at large – to flatten the diversity of human sexes into two diametrically opposed camps gives me pleasure' (p.23).

References

American Psychiatric Association (2013) *Diagnostic and Statistical Manual of Mental Disorders.* 5th Edition. Arlington: American Psychiatric Association.

Arfini, E.A.G. and Crocetti, D. (2015) 'I movimenti intersex/DSD in Italia. Stili di militanza e biomedicalizzazione del binarismo di genere' in M. Prearo (ed.), *Politiche dell'orgoglio. Sessualità, soggettività e movimenti sociali.* Pisa: Edizioni ETS, pp.139–159.

Arietti, L., Ballarin, C., Cuccio, G. and Marcasciano, P. (eds) (2010) *Elementi di critica trans.* Rome: manifestolibri.

AVEN Italia (2011). Available at: www.asexuality.org.it (accessed 8 November 2019).

Baird, V. (2001) *The No-Nonsense Guide to Sexual Diversity.* London: Verso.

Balocchi, M. (ed.) (2019) *Intersex: Antologia multidisciplinare.* Preface by L. Bernini. Pisa: Edizioni ETS.

Beachy, R. (2014) *Gay Berlin: Birthplace of a Modern Identity.* New York: Alfred A. Knopf.

Benjamin, H. (1953) 'Transvestitism and Transexualism', *International Journal of Sexology*, 7: 12–14.

Bergoglio, J.M. (2014) 'Discorso del Santo Padre Francesco alla delegazione dell'Ufficio Internazionale Cattolico dell'Infanzia' (BICE), *Bollettino della Sala stampa della Santa Sede*, 11 April.

Bergoglio, J.M. (2015) 'Udienza generale', *Bollettino della Sala stampa della Santa Sede*, 15 April.

Bergoglio, J.M. (2016) 'Discorso del Santo Padre Francesco in occasione dell'inaugurazione dell'anno giudiziario del tribunale della Rota romana', *Bollettino della Sala stampa della Santa Sede*, 22 January.

Bernini, L. (2014) 'Uno spettro si aggira per l'Europa ... Sugli usi e gli abusi del concetto di "gender"', *Cambio* 8: 81–90.

Bernini, L. (2016) 'La "teoria del gender", i "negazionisti" e la "fine della differenza sessuale"', *AG, About Gender* 10: 367–381.

Busi, B. (2016) 'Fare e disfare il sesso. Oltre il binarismo dei generi' in F. Zappino (ed.), *Il genere. Tra neoliberismo e neofondamentalismo.* Verona: Ombre Corte, pp.175–185.

Butler, J. (1990) *Gender Trouble: Feminism and the Subversion of Identity.* New York and London: Routledge.

Butler, J. (2004) 'The End of Sexual Difference', in J. Butler, *Undoing Gender.* New York and London: Routledge, pp.174–203.

Cauldwell, D.O. (1949) 'Psychopathia Trans-sexualis', *Sexology Magazine* 16: 274–280.

Chase, C. (1993) 'Intersexual Rights', *The Sciences* 33(4): 3.

Colapinto, J. (2000) *As Nature Made Him: The Boy Who Was Raised as a Girl.* New York and London: Harper Collins.

Crocetti, D. (2013) *L'invisibile intersex. Storie di corpi medicalizzati.* Pisa: Edizioni ETS.

Diamond, M. (1997) 'Sex Reassignment at Birth: A Long Term Review and Clinical Implications', *Archives of Pediatrics and Adolescent Medicine* 151(3): 298–304.

Donahoe, P.K. (1987) 'The Diagnosis and Treatment of Infants with Sexual Abnormalities', *Pediatric Clinics of North America* 34(5): 1333–1348.

Donahoe, P.K., Powell, D.M. and Lee, M.M. (1991) 'Clinical Management of Sexual Abnormalities', *Current Problems in Surgery* 28(8): 513–579.

Dreger, A.D. (1998) *Hermaphrodites and the Medical Invention of Sex.* Cambridge, MA: Harvard University Press.

Fausto-Sterling, A. (1993) 'The Five Sexes: Why Male and Female are Not Enough', *The Sciences* March/April: 20–24.

Fausto-Sterling, A. (2000) 'The Five Sexes, Revisited', *The Sciences* July/August: 19–23.

Feinberg, L. (1992) *Transgender Liberation: A Movement Whose Time Has Come.* New York: World View Forum.

Feinberg, L. (1993) *Stone Butch Blues.* Ithaca, NY: Firebrand Books.

Feinberg, L. (1996) *Transgender Warriors.* Boston: Beacon Press.

Ferrari, F., Ragaglia, E.M. and Rigliano, P. (2015) *Il genere. Una guida orientativa.* Torino: SIPSIS.

Foucault, M. (1976) *La volonté de savoir. Histoire de la sexualité* I. Paris: Éditions Gallimard.

Foucault, M. (1980) *Herculine Barbin: Being the Recently Discovered Memoirs of a Nineteenth Century French Hermaphrodite.* Translated by R. McDoughall. New York: Vintage Books.

Garbagnoli, S. (2014) '"L'ideologia del genere". L'irresistibile ascesa di un'invenzione retorica vaticana contro la denaturalizzazione dell'ordine sessuale', *AG, About Gender* 3(6): 250–263.

Goetz, A.M. and Baden, S. (1997) 'Who Needs [Sex] When You Can Have [Gender]? Conflicting Discourses on Gender at Beijing', *Feminist Review* 56(1): 3–25.

Goldschmidt, R. (1917) 'Intersexuality and the Endocrine Aspect of Sex', *Endocrinology* 1(4): 433–456.

Halberstam, J. (1998) *Female Masculinity*. Durham, NC: Duke University Press.

Havelock Ellis, H. and Symonds, J.A. (1897) *Sexual Inversion*. London: Wilson and McMillan.

Hirschfeld, M. (1910) *Die Transvestiten, eine Untersuchung über den erotischen Verkleidungstrieb mit umfangreichem causistischem und historischem Material*. Berlin: Medi-zinisher Verlag.

Hirschfeld, M. (1923) 'Die intersexuelle Konstitution', *Jahrbuch für sexuelle Zwishenstufen* 23: 3–27.

Hughes, I., Houk, C., Ahmed, F., Lee, P., LWPES, ESPE (2006) 'Consensus Statement on Management of Intersex Disorders', *Archives of Disease in Childhood* 118(2): 488–500.

Jones, T., Hart, B., Carpenter, M., Ansara, G., Leonard, W. and Lucke, J. (2015) *Intersex: Stories and Statistics from Australia*. Cambridge: Open Book Publisher.

Kessler, S.J. (1998) *Lessons from the Intersexed*. New Brunswick: Rutgers University Press.

Klebs, T.H. (1868) *Handbuch der pathologischen Anatomie*. Berlin: August Hirschwald.

Lorenzetti, A. (2013) *Diritti in transito. La condizione giuridica delle persone transessuali*. Milan: FrancoAngeli.

Marcasciano, P. (2002) *Tra le rose e le viole. La storia e le storie di transessuali e travestiti*. Rome: manifestolibri.

Marcasciano, P. (2006) 'Trans, donne e femministe' in T. Bertilotti, C. Galasso, A. Gissi and F. Lagorio (eds), *Altri femminismi*. Rome: manifestolibri, pp.37–54.

Marcasciano, P. (2008) *Favolose narranti. Storie di transessuali*. Rome: manifestolibri.

Marcasciano, P. (2014) *Antologaia. Vivere sognando e non sognare di vivere: i miei anni Settanta*. Rome: Alegre.

Money, J., Hampson, J.G. and Hampson, J.L. (1955) 'Hermaphroditism: Recommendations Concerning Assignment of Sex, Change of Sex, and Psychological Management', *Bulletin of The Johns Hopkins Hospital* 97(4): 284–300.

Money, J., Hampson, J.G. and Hampson, J.L. (1957) 'Imprinting and the Establishment of the Gender Role', *Archives of Neurology and Psychiatry* 77(3): 333–336.

Pasotti, M. (2017) '"Brutta sì, ma donna". Virginia Mauri alias Zefthe Akaira. Un celebre caso di ermafroditismo nell'Italia di fine Ottocento' in U. Grassi, V. Lagioia and G. Romagnani (eds), *Tribadi, sodomiti, invertite e invertiti, pederasti, femminelle, ermafroditi… Per una storia dell'omosessualità, della bisessualità e delle trasgressioni di genere in Italia*. Pisa: Edizioni ETS, pp.173–190.

Politi, M. (1995) 'La Chiesa si prepara alla guerra dei cinque sessi', *La Repubblica*, 20 May.

Presidenza del Consiglio dei Ministri, Comitato Nazionale per la Bioetica (2010) 'I disturbi della differenziazione sessuale nei minori: aspetti bioetici', 25 February.

Ratzinger, J.A. (2008) 'Discorso del Santo Padre Benedetto XVI alla Curia romana per la presentazione degli auguri natalizi', *Bollettino della Sala stampa della Santa Sede*, 22 December.

Ratzinger, J.A. (2012) 'Discorso del Santo Padre Benedetto XVI', *Bollettino della Sala stampa della Santa Sede*, 21 December.

Rich, A. (1980) 'Compulsory Heterosexuality and Lesbian Existence', *Signs: Journal of Women in Culture and Society* 5(4): 631–660.

Russo, G., Guarnieri, M.P., Peroni, P., Sgaramella, P., Greggio, N.A. and I. S.C. (2014) 'Opuscolo informativo'. Milano, San Raffaele Hospital – Scientific Institute for Shelter and Care – Paediatric-neonatal Operations Centre for Endocrinology of Childhood and Adolescence.

Scaramuzzi, I. (2015) 'Il Papa parla con i giovani di nozze e dei silenzi di Dio', *La stampa*, 21 March.

Stone, S. (2006) 'The Empire Strikes Back: A Posttranssexual Manifesto' in S. Stryker and S. Whittle (eds), *The Transgender Studies Reader*. New York and London: Routledge, pp.221–235.

Stryker, S. (2008) 'Transgender History, Homonormativity and Disciplinarity', *Radical History Review* 10: 145–157.

Stryker, S. (2015) 'Una storia del movimento transgender. Esperienza, omonormatività e pratiche disciplinari'. Translated by A.J. Habed. In M. Prearo (ed.), *Politiche dell'orgoglio. Sessualità, soggettività e movimenti sociali*. Pisa: Edizioni ETS, pp.38–56.

Stryker, S. and Whittle, S. (eds) (2006) *The Transgender Studies Reader*. New York and London: Routledge.

Stryker S., Whittle, S. and Azura, A.S. (eds) (2013) *The Transgender Studies Reader* 2. New York and London: Routledge.

von Krafft-Ebing, R. (1886) *Psychopathia sexualis. Eine klinisch-forensische Studie.* Stuttgart: Verlag von Fendinand Enke.

Westphal, O. (1869) 'Die conträre Sexualempfindung', *Archiv für Psychiatrie und Nervenkrenkheiten* 2: 73–108.

3   Elements of queer theory

Over the last twenty years or so, the Catholic Church and the traditionalist movements it inspires have been using expressions such as 'teoria del gender' [gender theory] or 'ideologia del gender' [gender ideology][1] to point to a caricatural version of feminist and queer theories. Indeed, by contesting patriarchy and the norms of the sex/gender binary system, feminist and queer theories directly clash with the naturalistic and heterosexist conception of sexual difference defended by the Vatican, and also with the pathologising and normalising instances that derive from it, which are still present in medical and psychological knowledge, as well as in legislation and in contemporary common sense. The severity of the clash goes much deeper than what the reassuring SIPSIS guide – along with other psychologists and progressive Italian intellectuals[2] – recognises, and from its perspective the Church is right to defend its own anthropological foundations. The Catholic campaign against the concept of 'gender', however, blatantly falsifies the facts when it condenses feminist and queer thought into a single theory or ideology that supposedly prescribes the manipulation of children with the ultimate goal of erasing sexual difference and producing a new transgender and/or five-sexes humanity. Both feminist and queer theories, in fact, exist in the plural, and constitute a vast field of political and academic debate, which only by way of extreme distortions can be compressed into a unitary ideology. Moreover, contemporary queer theories are an outcome of the methodological turn impressed by Foucault research on sexuality. Like most feminist theories, they can be considered critical non-normative political philosophies. Their intent, thus, is not to prescribe what everyone should do, but to take up the perspective of sexual minorities in order to denounce the impact that a long tradition of oppression, which the Church still aids and abets, has had on them. The exercise of an ontology of actuality, which we carried out in the previous chapter, is an example of how the queer critique of the power that acts on and through sexuality has no pretence to have absolute value, on the contrary, its value is one of contingency. Such critique is not static, but dynamic: it is nurtured by a lively debate between different opinions and is linked to the emergence of political subjectivities that self-organise into social movements. Queer theories are not exclusively academic. They are also, and above all, activist forms of knowledge, which have been developed by people directly involved in the politics of sexuality, and whose privileged interlocutors were the political movements of sexual minorities. There would be no queer theories without queer movements and, before them, sexual liberation movements.

Chapter 2, for example, insofar as it took into account the point of view of transgender movements, was not only based on the endorsement but also on the critique of Foucault's theory of the birth of modern homosexuality. It also showed how Fausto-Sterling's proposal for a new classification of the sexes evolved over time in dialogue with intersex movements. As critical political philosophies, queer theories are indeed an inexhaustible forum of debate on the relations between power and sexuality wherein, as Habermas would say, the logic of the best argument applies. The task of this chapter will be to reconstruct briefly, and perforce partially, a debate that has engaged them at least since the 1970s, identifying within it three different positions: revolutionary Freudo-Marxism, radical constructivism and antisocial theories. As critical political philosophies, queer theories also practice the art, theorised by Deleuze and Guattari, of inventing (and giving new meanings to) concepts. Two examples of this are the elaboration of the notion of 'transgender' and its multiple meanings, and the reclamation of the term 'intersex' as opposed to the medical acronym 'DSD' (Disorders of Sex Development). A third example is the re-appropriation of the term 'queer', and its political and theoretical use. 'Queer', as I will now try to show, is a polysemic term whose theoretical value derives precisely from the fact that it doesn't have a specific referent. Its worth consists in the fact that it has to be defined whenever it is used, or on the contrary in the fact that it can be used without having to be fully defined. Nowadays, participating in the debate about queer theories also means taking a position on the possible uses of the term. Not unlike the questions 'what is political philosophy?' and 'how does sexuality work?', the questions 'what does "queer" mean?', 'what are queer movements?' and 'what are queer theories?' cannot be answered unless some interpretative choices are made. In this instance I will trace the origin of queer philosophies back to a debate that took place in Europe two decades before the term 'Queer Theory' came into use in US universities. It will emerge clearly from this how Foucault laid the foundations for contemporary queer theories, by distancing himself from previous theories, which can only be improperly defined as 'queer', and in an equally improper and partial way can perhaps be compared – more than contemporary theories – to what the Catholic Church calls the theory/ideology of gender.

3.1 Queer movements and queer theories

Beginning in the nineteenth century, the term 'queer' was used in English as a derogatory slur against sexual minorities. Since the 1990s, first in the United States and then in the rest of the world, activists and thinkers have provocatively reclaimed the term as a signifier of political identity. Even before this resignification, however, the term had been traversed by a long history of semantic variations. The English 'queer' comes in fact from the Germanic adjective 'quer', which means 'transversal', 'diagonal', 'oblique', and which in turn comes from the Latin verb 'torqueo' ['to twist, to bend but also to torment']. 'Queer' can then be considered as the opposite of 'straight', which means both 'upright' and 'righteous' and by extension 'heterosexual' – since, in a regime of compulsory heterosexuality, heterosexuality is traditionally associated with moral rectitude. In Italian 'queer' can be translated with 'storto' ['crooked'], 'strano' ['strange'], 'strambo' ['weird'], 'bizzarro' ['odd'], 'bislacco' ['quirky'], but its equivalents are insults such as 'faggot' ['frocio'], 'poof' ['finocchio'], 'bugger' ['culattone'], although these only apply to men, whereas in English 'queer' can also be used against women.

Indeterminacy and versatility of both connotation and denotation remain also in the term's current theoretical deployment. The fact that 'queer' is a floating signifier, however, does not imply that it is an empty signifier, or open to any meaning whatsoever. Both in its theoretical and activist usages, the term fluctuates around a series of political anchoring points, which coalesce not only in the fight against sexism, male chauvinism, homophobia, transphobia, biphobia, but also in the critique of the sex/gender binary system, heteronormativity (the 'ideology' of compulsory heterosexuality[3]) and of those normative apparatuses that queer theories have been analysing since the early 2000s through such concepts as 'homonormativity', 'trans-normativity' and 'homonationalism'.[4]

Queer activism and queer thought differ from lesbian, gay and mainstream transgender activism and thought. On the one hand, they denounce that sexual minority movements and communities also produce their own normative models, exclusion mechanisms and hierarchical orders within themselves. On the other hand, they also argue that the integration of sexual minorities in neoliberal societies risks being carried out at the expense of other minorities. The spread of the acronym GLBT (gay, lesbian, bisexual, transgender, later replaced by LGBT) in the 1990s, for example, coincided with the emergence of civil rights campaigns for same-sex couples. In the United States and in Europe, these campaigns gave visibility especially to white, wealthy, able-bodied and cisgender gay couples with sufficiently 'manly' gender expression – followed by white, able-bodied and cisgender lesbian couples with sufficiently 'feminine' gender expression.

The concept of homonormativity refers, indeed, to the process through which LGBT communities and movements, which should have expressed the demands of all sexual minorities indicated by the LGBT acronym, have instead mostly been represented by a respectable and reassuring image of homosexuality, primarily male. And such image has produced as politically incorrect – and thus no longer publicly acceptable – other expressions of homosexuality, such as gay male effeminacy and lesbian masculinity; or the experimentation of lifestyles that diverge from a stable affective union between two partners; or, further still, disability and poverty among LGBT people and the fact that some of them belong to subordinate classes, racialised communities, movements fighting against neoliberalism. The social recognition of gays and lesbians has therefore been obtained at the price of making lesbians partially invisible, of deciding not to represent some gays and lesbians, and especially at the price of gay and lesbian movements distancing themselves not only from the radical left, but also from transgender and intersex movements – something which has paradoxically occurred by adding an ineffective T (and more recently, in some cases, the letter I and even the letter Q for queer and a + for other subjectivities, or other letters: A for asexual, P for pansexual, a second Q for questioning …) after the other letters of the acronym. On the other hand, transgender and intersex/DSD movements themselves are not immune from internal forms of discriminatory normativity: in both cases, it is mainly white, able, wealthy and educated people who obtain visibility and occupy leadership roles. In transgender movements, moreover, there are those who favour a respectable image of the good productive transgender citizen against the stereotypical association of transgenderism with immigration and sex work; there are also those who claim the status of 'real man' or 'real woman' because they aesthetically approximate cisgender and heterosexual standards of masculinity and femininity, and/or because they have undergone genital surgery. Finally, in intersex/DSD movements there are also those who prefer to publicly present themselves as male or female, cisgender and heterosexual, and as carriers of one of the different 'syndromes' that medicine classifies as DSD, rather than affiliate themselves as intersex people with the LGBTQI+ movements. However, homonormativity, transnormativity[5] and these attitudes, expressed not only by individuals but also by intersex/DSD[6] groups, are clearly in contrast with the critique of the sex/gender binary system and of compulsory heterosexuality, and support, as Lisa Duggan (2004) states, the 'dominant heteronormative institutions' (such as marriage). By detaching the claims of sexual minorities from the critique against injustices caused by racialisation processes and class differences, they also fuel a depoliticised and privatised interpretation of sexuality, 'anchored in domesticity and consumption' (p.50). To this we must add that since 11 September 2001 the rights of sexual minorities (and in particular the rights of the white, wealthy, cisgender gay men mentioned above) are increasingly being used in nationalist rhetoric that juxtaposes

North American and European neoliberal culture to the rest of the world, in order to justify the introduction of anti-Islamic and anti-immigration policies. Also this phenomenon – which Jasbir Puar (2007) called 'homonationalism' – is thus revealing of how the integration of sexual minorities in heterosexual and neoliberal societies does not only damage other minorities (Muslims, migrants, people who are less well-off, racialised people, disabled and/or anti-capitalist people), but sexual minorities themselves (LGBTI+ Muslims, LGBTI+ migrants, LGBTI+ people who are less well-off, LGBTI+ racialised people, LGBTI+ disabled and/or anti-capitalist people).[7]

The concepts of homonormativity, transnormativity and homonationalism are therefore tools developed by contemporary queer theories in order to exert a political critique of the desire of sexual minorities to assimilate. The history of this critique, however, starts long before the elaboration of these concepts, and also before the theoretical and political re-signification of the term 'queer' itself. In the next pages I will improperly include Foucault's constructivism and Mieli's Freudo-Marxism in a discussion of queer theories, although both precede the introduction of the expression 'queer theories'. I do this because the two authors, despite some major differences, do not limit themselves to calling for the integration of sexual minorities in the heterosexual and neoliberal society, but take issue with the very functioning of the heterosexual and neoliberal society and call into question the criteria separating sexual minorities from the heterosexual majority. Not only constructivism (an exercise of which I performed in the second chapter), but also Freudo-Marxism problematises the functioning of contemporary sexuality, challenges the naturalisation of the categories which form the sex-gender-sexual orientation system and denounces how, through them, sexual desires and behaviours are regulated, disciplined and subordinated to productive and reproductive requirements. Both schools of thought can be rightly considered 'queer theories', although they precede the inception of Queer Theory as its own field of study. The one I will reconstruct below, however, is only one of the many possible genealogies of such a field, alongside which there are others. In the United States, for example, the search for origins present in the debate in the fields of black queer studies and queer of colour critique[8] now passes with increasing frequency through a queer rereading not only of Cherrie Moraga (1983) and Gloria Anzaldùa's (1987) chicana feminisms, but also of Hortense Spillers's (1987) black feminism, and even through Frantz Fanon's anti-racist critique (Macharia, 2013). Despite being informed by male chauvinism and homophobia,[9] Fanon's 1952 essay *Black Skin, White Masks* highlights how colonial modernity established an equivalence between the 'black body' and genitality, producing a hypersexualisation of black men, which makes it impossible for them to fully identify with the male gender, represented by white men.

Similarly, in her 1987 article 'Mama's Baby, Papa's Maybe: An American Grammar Book', Spillers highlights how in the United States slavery has deprived black women of their female subjectivity, making their bodies devoid of gender identity. Before 1989 then – when legal scholar Kimberlé Crenshaw (1989) coined the term 'intersectionality' to name the need to consider at once determining factors such as race, class and gender in order to offer fair pronouncements on discriminatory processes – both Fanon and Spillers assumed race as the framing concept through which to perceive the historical and arbitrary dimension of the sex/gender binary system and its differential and uneven functioning in relation to the colour of one's skin. The problematisation of the links between race, class and sexuality, and the burdensome legacy of slavery in the United States, was in fact of fundamental importance to the birth of contemporary queer theories between the late 1980s and the early 1990s. As for the birth of queer movements, along with the marks left by the US legacy of slavery, another historical determining factor that cannot be forgotten, is the outbreak of the AIDS pandemic.

The history of the syndrome, of its spread and its social perception, is strongly marked by factors such as class, race and nationality (Geazry, 2014). And this is still the case. Today, in many countries, antiretroviral therapies that slow down or stop the progress of the disease are accessible only to a privileged few. In Sub-Saharan Africa, in particular, the AIDS infection continues to have a catastrophic impact. Since its inception, moreover, the disease has lent itself to stigmatising instrumentalisations. It suffices to remind the reader that between 1981, when the first case was diagnosed, and 1982, when the AIDS acronym (Acquired Immune Deficiency Syndrome) was coined, the US Centers for Disease Control and Prevention named it 'The 4H Disease', after the main four communities affected by it: Haemophiliacs, Heroin users, Haitians and

Homosexuals. During the same period, the American press pre-ferred instead to name it 'GRID': *Gay-Related Immune Deficiency* (Altman, 1986). Gay men and transgender women from the gay communities of New York and San Francisco were indeed among the people initially most affected by the disease in the United States. More importantly though, both gay men and transgender women were the subjects for which the diagnosis would more promptly translate into stigma. Starting in the early 1980s, a vicious campaign of criminalisation swept through not only the United States, but also Europe and the rest of the world,[10] targeting their 'lifestyles', their sexual promiscuity and their sexual practices. In addition to being marked by class and race, the history of AIDS concerns of course sex, gender and sexual orientation. And this is why it is closely linked to the history of queer political subjectivation. On 20 March 1990, a group of approximately sixty HIV+ activists foun-ded the first protest group on the grounds of the Lesbian, Gay, Bisexual and Transgender Community Services Center in New York. Among the potential names of the new association, 'Queer Nation', a name which had initially circulated, was officially approved in the assembly of 17 May, and later adopted by similar groups in San Francisco and other US cities. This is the first move-ment that reclaims the insult 'queer' for its own political identity, renewing thus the style of militancy in the LGBT movements. The actions of the New York group immediately acquired an ironic, provocative and verbally aggressive profile, and often sought to publicly display the existence of untamed minoritised sexual sub-jectivities, who refused to be confined to the invisibility to which heterosexual societies had always condemned them, and which AIDS and its social perception had only worsened. On the evening of 13 April 1990, for example, a small crowd of lesbians and gays shocked the straight customers of a club in the Village by flaunting homosexual affection. On 26 April, some Queer Nation activists protested against homophobic attacks by hanging on top of the sign of another club in the area a large banner with the slogan 'Dykes and fags bash back!', which two days later was paraded around the neighbourhood during an unauthorised march. Other slogans later used by the group were 'We're here! We're queer! Get used to this!' and 'Out of the closets and into the streets!'.

Instead of reacting to the wave of homo-trans-bi-phobia triggered by the AIDS crisis by presenting themselves as victims of the disease in need of state protection and eager to integrate into the state as 'good' citizens, the activists of Queer Nation preferred to present themselves as 'bad' people, as troublesome, noisy, deviant subjects, that is, as queer, as those faggots and dykes who, with their lifestyles and sexual practices, provoked disgust among right-thinking citizens. Instead of promoting a reassuring image of homosexuality and transgenderism, they chose to enact – as Butler would say – a 'reworking of [their own] abjection into political agency' (1993, p.21), and to challenge bourgeois respectability. In so doing, they made reference to the origins of the gay liberation movement. Already in the 1950s, in fact, there were gay and lesbian assimilationist movements in the United States that were committed to spreading a respectable image of homosexuality.[11] However, on the night of 27 June 1969, it wasn't white gay men in their suits and ties and white lesbians in their blazers who rebelled against New York's police raids, but the multiracial customers of an infamous club, the Stonewall Inn. It was drag queens, transgender sex workers in their flashy outfits, butch lesbians in biker jackets and effeminate gay hustlers dancing on the tables in their underwear who started the riot.[12] As the story goes, it was transgender activist of Puerto Rican and Venezuelan origin, Sylvia Rivera, who started the clashes by throwing an empty bottle of gin at a policeman – most probably, it was Stormé DeLarverie, a butch lesbian and drag king, born of a black mother and a white father, who stirred up the crowd to fight. In any case, in the years following, Rivera went on to found STAR (Street Transvestite Action Revolutionaries), while other activists – among whom black drag queen Marcia P. Johnson – constituted the GLF (Gay Liberation Front), whose name is modelled after the ALF (Algerian Liberation Front). Since then LGBTQI+ movements around the world celebrate 28 June as their pride day, but it is especially queer movements that have preserved the memory of the revolt and have taken the legacy of those first radical and revolutionary groups. On the occasion of the commemorative parade in New York in 1990, Queer Nation distributed its own manifesto, inviting sexual minorities to form an 'army' to fight against 'straight' oppression, of which the public opinion's reaction to the AIDS crisis was but one manifestation. The association did not ask the State to carve out islands of tolerance in the private sphere according to the liberal model of a politics of rights, but proposed to subvert heterosexual society by making every public space a 'lesbian and gay space' in which to live a 'different kind of life':

> Being queer is not about a right to privacy; it is about the freedom to be public, to just be who we are. It means everyday fighting oppression, homophobia, racism, misogyny, the bigotry of religious hypocrites and our own self-hatred. (We have been carefully taught to hate ourselves.) And now of course it means fighting a virus as well, and all those homo-haters who are using AIDS to wipe us off the face of the earth. Being queer means leading a different sort of life. It's not about the mainstream, profit-margins, patriotism, patriarchy or being assimilated. It's not about executive directors, privilege and elitism. It's about being on the margins, defining ourselves; it's about gender-fuck and secrets, what's beneath the belt and deep inside the heart; it's about the night. Being queer is 'grass roots' because we know that everyone of us, every body, every cunt, every heart and ass and dick is a world of pleasure waiting to be explored. Everyone of us is a world of infinite possibility. We are an army because we have to be. We are an army because we are so powerful. (We have so much to fight for; we are the most precious of endangered species.) And we are an army of lovers because it is we who know what love is. Desire and lust, too. We invented them. We come out of the closet, face the rejection of society, face firing squads, just to love each other! Every time we fuck, we win. We must fight for ourselves (no else is going to do it) and if in that process we bring greater freedom to the world at large then great ... Let's make every space a Lesbian and Gay space.[13]
>
> (Queer Nation Manifesto)

The provocative spirit of these words, such as the outburst of anger and pride, which was the spark that ignited the Stonewall revolt, is still alive and well in some contemporary movements. To this day, and in Italy too, self-defining as 'queer' are many radical political groups and collectives who are not satisfied with demanding the protection of the State against the discrimination they suffer, and neither with demanding their integration into the heterosexual social order based on the family (the right to marry, to adopt, to getting access to assisted reproduction technologies) or within the capitalist economy (through the creation of LGBT market niches, the organisation of an LGBT entertainment industry, the exploitation of sexual diversity in corporate management). These groups promote instead oppositional politics and lifestyles based on the refusal of homonormativity, transnormativity, homonationalism and neoliberalism.[14] In Italy, for example, up to now the adjective queer has been adopted by those factions of the LGBT movements that fight with steadfast resolution – and according to some with extremist resolution – for the self-determination of transgender people, sex workers, intersex, bisexual and asexual people, migrant and racialised people; and to denounce the fallout effects that neoliberal policies, work precarisation and the economic crisis that began in 2008 have had on the lives of students, workers and the unemployed. Queer politics is also characterised by the fact that it is anchored in the present rather than projected into the future, as it does not have definitive objectives (such as social integration through equal family rights) but always only partial ones. Queer politics does not follow pre-established strategies or programmes but is redefined each time by the contingency of its struggles.

Some of these characteristics, as I have already anticipated, are also found in most queer theories. Since they are mostly critical and non-normative, these theories do not translate into elaborate projects for the construction of future societies in which sexual minorities can be perfectly integrated. On the contrary, they translate into practices of thought focused on a critique of the present society. In academia, it was Teresa de Lauretis who first claimed to have put the adjective 'queer' beside the noun 'theory'. In what follows she explains the meaning of her provocation:

When I coined the expression 'Queer Theory' for a conference on homosexuality held at my own university in 1990, the term queer (strange, weird, quirky) had been used for more than a century as a derogatory term to designate a homosexual person. However, it had already been repurposed and reclaimed by the gay liberation movement and was proudly used by openly declared homosexual men and women. In defining the topic of the conference I was organizing with those words instead of, for example, 'gay and lesbian sexuality', I wanted to open a space to discuss and interrogate, first of all, the idea that female and male homosexuality were the same form of sexuality, independent of gender. Secondly, I also wanted to throw into question the idea that homosexuality could be identified exclusively by way of contrasting it with heterosexuality (which thing, however, feminist studies had clearly demonstrated was differentiated in female and male heterosexuality).

(de Lauretis, 1999, pp.104–105, translated by M. Baldo and E. Basile)

Teresa de Lauretis makes reference here to the University of Santa Cruz (California), and to the conference that took place there in February 1990. The conference proceedings were published the following year as part of a thematic volume of the journal *differences*, edited by de Lauretis herself, and her own paper, 'Queer Theory: Lesbian and Gay Sexualities: An Introduction', became the volume's opening essay. Her intention was not to introduce a new, univocal perspective on sexuality and homosexuality, but to multiply the range of perspectives on standards in place in the social and academic interpretation of sexuality at the time, by throwing into question what had become common sense. How has it come to be that in American culture, and particularly in the academy, we take for granted the existence of a universal homosexual condition that supposedly unites gays and lesbians? What hegemonic processes of exclusion and erasure are at play here? Why is gender considered irrelevant to sexuality, and why aren't class and racial differences taken into account as provoking fractures also within lesbian and gay communities? Why are gay and lesbian identities understood as being determined exclusively by the fact that they are not heterosexual in a heterosexist society? By dedicating a conference to Queer Theory rather than Gay and Lesbian Studies, de Lauretis was not intending to provide quick and easy answers to these questions. Rather, her aim was to create a space in which these questions could still be asked, one, which would escape the grip not only of heteronormativity, but also of the homonormativity that is the product of the neoliberal way of life:

The project of the conference was based on the speculative premise that homosexuality is no longer to be seen simply as marginal with regard to a dominant, stable form of sexuality (heterosexuality) against which it would be defined either by opposition or by homology. In other words, it is no longer to be seen either as merely transgressive or deviant vis-a-vis a proper, natural sexuality (i.e., institutionalized reproductive sexuality), according to the older, pathological model, or as just another, optional 'life-style,' according to the model of contemporary North American pluralism ... [T]he conference was intended to articulate the terms in which lesbian and gay sexualities may be understood and imaged [*sic*] as forms of resistance to cultural homogenization, counteracting dominant discourses with other constructions of the subject in culture. It was my hope that the conference would also problematize some of the discursive constructions and constructed silences in the emergent field of 'gay and lesbian studies,' and would further explore questions that have as yet been barely broached, such as the respective and/or common grounding of current discourses and practices of homo-sexualities in relation to gender and to race, with their attendant differences of class or ethnic culture, generational, geographical, and socio-political location ... And hence the title of the conference and of this issue of *differences*: 'Queer Theory' conveys a double emphasis – on the conceptual and speculative work involved in discourse production, and on the necessary critical work of deconstructing our own discourses and their constructed silences ... The term 'queer,' juxtaposed to the 'lesbian and gay' of the subtitle, is intended to mark a certain critical distance from the latter, by now established and often convenient, formula. For the phrase 'lesbian and gay' or 'gay and lesbian' has become the standard way of referring to what only a few years ago used to be simply 'gay' (e.g., the gay community, the gay liberation movement) or, just a few years earlier still, 'homosexual'.

(1991, pp.iii–iv, italics added)

In the second note of the introduction to the thematic volume of *differences*, de Lauretis is keen to underscore the fact that at the time of the conference she was not aware of the existence of Queer

Nation, from which she distances herself, by stating that 'there is in fact very little in common between Queer Nation and this *queer theory*' (de Lauretis, 1999, p.xvii, italics added). She herself, however, does identify in the AIDS crisis and the anti-homosexual panic that ensued from it one of the reasons why a gay and lesbian alliance is necessary, even in spite of their differences. She also seems to describe Queer Nation's typical style of activism when she theorises an activism that

> rather than marking the limits of the social space by designating a place at the edge of culture … acts as an agency of social process whose mode of functioning is both interactive and yet resistant, both participatory and yet distinct, claiming at once equality and difference, demanding political representation while insisting on its material and historical specificity.
>
> (de Lauretis, 1991, p.iii)

In any case, 1990 – the same year in which Queer Nation was founded in New York and in which the conference organised by de Lauretis took place in Santa Cruz – is also the year of publication of two fundamental texts that provide the occasion for another misrecognition. Although neither Eve Kosofsky Sedgwick's (1990) *Epistemology of the Closet* nor *Gender Trouble: Feminism and the Subversion of Identity* (1999 [1990]) by Judith Butler contain the expression 'queer theory', the two books continue today to be often celebrated as the founding texts of Queer Theory[15] within cultural studies and political philosophy, as their wide dissemination and fame ended up overshadowing Teresa de Lauretis's conference. However, as I have anticipated, in my opinion, and not solely my own, we need to go further back in time if we want to delineate the origins of queer *theories*. Indeed, Foucault's thought is a fundamental common reference among de Lauretis, Sedgwick and Butler. Foucault, who died of AIDS at the age of fifty-seven in 1984, never spoke of queer theories, nor could he have heard of them; however, the publication of *La volonté de savoir* in 1976 did, if not initiate, at least give structure to a method of critical enquiry on sexuality that led from the 1990s onward to the emergence of a field of research wherein queer theories as we know them today came to be inscribed. In a 1993 essay, which was included the following year in the volume *Tendencies* (Sedgwick, 1994), Sedgwick outlines a

definition of 'queer' using words in which one can easily recognise the
French philosopher's influence:

> That's one of the things that 'queer' can refer to: the open mesh
> of possibilities, gaps, overlaps, dissonances and resonances,
> lapses and excesses of meaning when the constituent elements
> of anyone's gender, of anyone's sexuality aren't made (or *can't
> be* made) to signify monolithically. The experimental linguistic,
> epistemological, representational, political adventures attaching
> to the very many of us who may at times be moved to describe
> ourselves as (among many other possibilities) pushy femmes,
> radical faeries, fantasists, drags, clones, leatherfolk, ladies in
> tuxedos, feminist women or feminist men, masturbators, bull-
> daggers, divas, Snap! queens, butch bottoms, storytellers,
> transsexuals, aunties, wannabes, lesbian-identified men or les-
> bians who sleep with men, or … people able to relish, learn
> from, or identify with such … At the same time, a lot of the
> most exciting recent work around 'queer' spins the term out-
> ward along dimensions that can't be subsumed under gender
> and sexuality at all: the ways that race, ethnicity, postcolonial
> nationality criss-cross with these *and other* identity-constitut-
> ing, identity-fracturing discourses, for example.
>
> (1994, pp.8–9)

Queer theories are critical philosophies in the sense understood by
Foucault. They are exercises in an ontology of actuality, acts of
insubordination and disobedience through which unruly subjects distance themselves from the power/knowledge regime that defines and
governs their sexuality, experimenting as a result with disidentifica-
tions and new precarious identities. Queer theories are exercises in an
ontology of the self: ascetic exercises that have transformative effects
on those who practice them. At the same time, the theories themselves emerge from these exercises, from those points of rupture that
occur when individuals and movements resist the power/knowledge
regime that defines and governs their sexualities, producing in it
cracks and gaps from which such regime becomes more easily observable. Foucault inaugurates queer theories because his critical thought
on sexuality is an invitation to question the 'naturalness' and the
'stability' of terms such as 'male', 'female', 'man', 'woman',

'heterosexual', 'homosexual', 'transsexual', 'DSD', in short to question the way we define ourselves and conduct our life. Foucault's method invites us to ask questions such as: Who are we today? Who are we when we define ourselves through these terms? How did we come to think of our sexuality through them? What vectors of power do these terms relay? How do these terms intersect with other variables of identity, with other vectors of power, such as class, race, nationality, dis/ability? Do these terms really represent us? And whom do they really represent? What is the effect, for example, on a female transgender migrant prostitute of the social respectability that lesbians and gays have earned in certain states and in certain circles, by playing the part of the good citizens who demand the right to marry? And how are these terms redefined by historical contingencies? Not only by the acquisition of full marriage rights for lesbians and gays in some States (though not in Italy at the time of this writing), but, even earlier by the AIDS crisis, the fall of the Berlin Wall, 11 September or the 2008 economic crisis? And what other possibilities do we have to name our sexuality starting from a critique of these terms? The list of dissident sexualities compiled by Sedgwick will make some people smile for its oddity, but in others it will have the liberating effect of having them recognise in that oddity their queerness, the opening up of a space for new ways of life and new ways of thinking.

3.2 Revolutionary Freudo-Marxism and radical constructivism

In the first chapter I provisionally defined queer theories as critical political philosophies that question the relationship between power and sexuality, adopting a sexual minorities' perspective.[16] I also defined philosophy in different ways, borrowing from Petrucciani (and from Habermas) the idea that philosophy is an open-ended and endless discussion, in which from time to time, but always provisionally, the best argument prevails. It will not be surprising, therefore, that the theorisations on sexuality by a forerunner of queer theories such as Foucault are themselves part of a polemic against a set of political doctrines which, by virtue of this very same polemic, I propose to place at the origin – one of the possible origins – of the queer debate, although such polemic largely precedes the latter. I am referring to what is known as Freudo-Marxism, that is, to the theories of *The Sexual Revolution* developed back in the 1930s by Wilhelm Reich (1927/1973, 1936/1974), and taken up in the 1950s by Herbert Marcuse (1955, 1964), and subsequently spread widely among the new protest movements of the left during the 1970s. In Italy, it was Mario Mieli who inserted himself in this tradition by providing a 'particularly queer' version of it, through his book *Towards a Gay Communism: Elements of Homosexual Critique*. As the name suggests, Freudo-Marxism associates the revolutionary instances of Marxism with the liberation potentials of Freudian theories, offering a critique of capitalist society and of sexual repression at the same time. Indeed, this school of thought theorises the impact of power on sexuality essentially, although not exclusively, in the form of repression, and conceives sexuality mainly as a repressed desire that asks to be liberated.

For Freud, the repression and sublimation not only of desires but also of sexual drives is a necessary aspect of the psychosexual development of each individual, so that we can learn the norms and conventions that allow us to live together. It is precisely the impossibility of expressing our total self within society that causes our *civilised discontent*, which Freud (1930/2002) considers *inevitable* and therefore investigates from an a-historical perspective. Freudo-Marxist authors denounce, instead, the arbitrariness of the modes of sexual repression enforced in the wake of capitalism, arguing that the latter represses desire in order to sublimate its energy into labour power aimed at the production and reproduction of an alienated society.[17] They also claim that overthrowing the repressive institutions of the bourgeois society would lead to a free, peaceful, non-competitive society, in which human beings could experience full happiness, instead of discomfort. As for the contents of this promise of happiness, however, the authors disagree. For Reich, a liberated sexuality will be expressed through heterosexual (and thus potentially reproductive) acts between adult men and women, as homosexuality is considered the result of an 'unnatural' sexual development.[18]

Marcuse on the other hand, wishes for the thriving of the kind infantile sexuality described by Freud in the *Three Essays on the Theory of Sexuality*: a sexuality, that is, not aimed at reproduction, and therefore not focused on genitals, but widespread all over the body's surface and oriented to the search for pleasure in multiple directions. Following Freud, Marcuse calls this sexuality 'poly-morphous-perverse' (1955, p.49).[19] At the same time, however, he is keen to disprove 'the expectation that instinctual liberation can lead only to a society of sex maniacs – that is, to no society' (p.201). In his opinion, in a liberated society sexual desire would undergo a process of non-repressive sublimation, which would partially con-vert it into Eros, that is, into a non-alienated social bond, consonant with the pursuit of pleasure. In such a society neither reproduction nor production would fail, and labour 'would be assimilated to play – the free play of human faculties' (p.214). As an example of the difference between repressive and non-repressive sublimation, Marcuse quotes *Group Psychology and the Analysis of the Ego* by Freud (1921/1959), according to whom all social bonds are erotic bonds, as in the following: '"sexual love for women" as well as "desexualized, sublimated, homosexual love for other men" here appear as instinctual sources of an enduring and expanding culture' (Marcuse, 1955, p.207). *Towards a Gay Communism: Elements of a Homosexual Critique* has many points in common with Marcuse's thought, but Mieli's defence of homosexuality is much more radical, and is combined with a representation of sexual revolution in which there is very little that is sublimated. Marcuse argues, in passing, that 'within the historical dynamic of the instinct, for example, coprophilia and homosexuality have a very different place and function' (p.203), meaning, if I understand correctly, that the repression of the former is necessary for civilisation, whereas the repression of the latter is not. Mieli – who was one of the founders in the 1970s of the Italian homosexual liberation movement [20] – argues, however, that it is no coincidence that the two 'perversions' trigger a similar disgust, and links the liberation of one to that of the other:

> Heterosexual males also fear the excremental aura of anal intercourse. 'But Love has pitched its mansion in/The place of excrement' (Yeats). We gays know this very well, and our condition is most close to the joyous redemption of shit – if we have not already attained this. Even as far as shit is concerned, too, the repressive disgust conceals a rich enjoyment.
>
> (1977/2018, p.149)

The critique of sexual repression and capitalist economy is also accompanied in Mieli by a critique of that norm – 'Norm', actually, to quote him correctly – which a few years after the publication of *Towards a Gay Communism* Adrienne Rich will teach us to call 'compulsory heterosexuality' (Rich, 1980).[21] Indeed, he reminds us that in Freud the concept of 'perverse polymorphism' is synonymous with 'original bisexuality', which is understood not as the coexistence of heterosexual and homosexual desire, but as the co-presence of masculine and feminine gender identifications. Mieli also highlights the fact that when Marcuse quotes Freud in this regard, without questioning his thought, he inherits an understanding of homosexuality that is bound to the inversion model and is infused with heterosexism – that is, with the idea that desire is always and only heterosexual, and therefore those who are sexually attracted to a person of the same sex need to identify, at least partially, with the gender opposite to the one assigned at birth. To this Marcusian thesis Mieli responds by positing an equivalence between 'perverse polymorphism' and what he calls 'transsexuality' (which, following Leslie Feinberg,[22] we would today be likely to call 'transgenderism', and which activist Peter Boom,[23] following a few passages by Mieli himself, has instead renamed as 'pansexuality'). For Mieli 'transsexuality' is a primary kind of desire, which precedes the difference between male and female, and therefore between heterosexuality and homosexuality:

> The original and far-reaching theory of bisexuality or 'ambisexuality' (Ferenczi) does not clarify the causes of so-called 'sexual inversion', but it does justify it. According to Otto Weininger, author of *Sex and Character* (1903) and a keen upholder of the theory of bisexuality, homosexuality is neither a vice nor unnatural, given that any man, being also female, can equally well desire another man (who is himself also a woman), just as any woman, being at the same time male, can equally well desire another woman (who is also a man). But this justification of homosexuality is not good enough (and in fact falls fully within the essentially reactionary perspective of tolerance). Weininger simply tried to fit homoeroticism into the bipolar pattern of heterosexuality. Homosexuality is explained in terms of heterosexual categories. I believe, rather, that homosexuality

contains, among its secrets, the possibility of understanding psychobiological hermaphroditism not as something *bi*-sexual, but rather as erotic in a new (and also very old) sense, as polysexual, transsexual. The heterosexual categories are based on a rejection of the underlying hermaphrodism, on the submission of the body to the neurotic directives of the censored mind, on an ego-istic vision of the world-of-life as determined by the repression of woman and Eros, by compulsory sexual morality, by the negation of human community and by individualistic atomisation. It is no good trying to use the bisexual and therefore heterosexual categories of our alienated reason, superimposed on the latent and the repressed, to plumb the depths, for we shall only fail to appreciate the full scope of the repression that chains us to the status quo. We revolutionary gays want rather to raise ourselves to transsexuality, as a concrete process of liberation.

(1977/2018, pp.19–20)

According to Mieli, therefore, both heterosexuality and homosexuality are the result of a mutilation in the subject.[24] He coins the term 'educastration' (p.5) to indicate the repressive educational process through which the heterosexual majority acquires a gender and a sexual orientation, presumably consistent both with the sex assigned at birth and with the transformation of homosexual desire into homophobic contempt. Mieli also confesses that he does not understand the reason why a misfit minority of people, impervious to the educastration they are nonetheless subjected to, develop a homosexual identity,[25] give up heterosexual desire and assume the social role of scapegoats: a role that is functional to the release, in the form of violence, of the homoerotic desires of heterosexual men. Thus, according to Mieli, despite being its transgression, homosexuality also confirms the Norm[26] in contemporary alienated societies. In his view, it is because of this that the psychological characteristic of most homosexuals is a sacrificial masochism (1977/2018, p.130).

Mieli distances himself from Marcuse also on another issue, in regard to which he believes his theory is 'out of date', paving thus the way for queer contemporary reflections on the ability by neoliberal policies to domesticate and co-opt minority subjects.[27] For the young

Italian philosopher and activist, advanced capitalism does not limit itself to banishing perversions. It also turns them into profit:

> Today it is clear that our society makes very good use of the 'perversions'; you need only go into a newsagent or to the cinema to be made well aware of this. 'Perversion' is sold both wholesale and retail; it is studied, classified, valued, marketed, accepted, discussed. It becomes a fashion, going in and out of style. It becomes culture, science, printed-paper, and money – if not, then who would publish this book? The unconscious is sold in slices over the butcher's counter. If for millennia, therefore, societies have repressed the so-called 'perverse' components of Eros in order to sublimate them in labour, the present system liberalises these 'perversions' with a view to their further exploitation in the economic sphere, and to subordinating all erotic tendencies to the goals of production and consumption. This liberalisation, as I have already argued, is functional only to a commodification in the deadly purposes of capital. Repressed 'perversion', then, no longer provides simply the energy required for labour, but is also to be found, fetishised, in the alienating product of alienated labour, which capital puts on the market in reified form.
>
> (p.224)

Nonetheless, Mieli trusts that gays and lesbians can free themselves both from their masochism and from the commodification of their 'perversion' in order to accomplish, together with feminist women, that sexual revolution whose outcomes will be 'the discovery and progressive liberation of the transsexuality of the subject', 'the negation of the polarity between the sexes', the advent of 'the new man-woman, or far more likely, woman-man' (1977/2018, p.254) who will live the fullness of desire beyond all identitarian enclosures. If there is, then, in the genealogy of queer theories that I am proposing, a moment in which such genealogy touches on the themes that are attributed to 'gender ideology', I have just reached it. In a 1981 essay 'One is not born a woman', Monique Wittig re-elaborates Marxist materialism in order to claim that the ultimate aim of the feminist struggle can only be 'the destruction of heterosexuality as a social system which is based on the oppression of women by men and which produces the doctrine of the difference between the sexes to justify this oppression' (1992, p.20).[28] Already in 1977, Mieli was making use of Freudo-Marxism to support a similar thesis. In addition, he also sketches an outline of the liberated subject, who, unlike the subject theorised by Marcuse, is a true polymorphous pervert: neither man nor woman (though more woman than man), transsexual, anal, coprophagous and even paedophile (1977/2018, p.54);[29] a delusional subject, who instead of sublimating or postponing their desires, fulfils them immediately, to the point of falling in a state of blissful schizophrenia (p.195).[30]

Truth be told, then, Mieli offers plenty of fodder for critique to the opponents of so-called 'gender ideology'. This said, I'd like to remind the reader that the inclusion of Freudo-Marxism in a genealogy of queer theories is possible primarily because of the *critique* that Foucault's operated of it. It was this critique that inaugurated a new way of thinking about the relationship between power and sexuality, which is what de Lauretis, Sedgwick and Butler draw upon. With a few exceptions – among which is James Penney (2013), who proposes to *abandon* queer theory and return to Freudo-Marxism, by making explicit reference to the thought of Mario Mieli and Guy Hocquenghem – contemporary queer theories do not offer solutions but instead raise problems (or 'trouble', as in the title of Butler's famous book). They also juxtapose their own scepticism against the belief in the existence of an essential foundation for the subject. The space occupied by desire in Mieli's thinking remains empty after Foucault. Even though Mieli's theorisations partially resonate with the return to psychoanalysis in some recent antisocial theories (which in turn engage in a critique of Foucault's constructivism), these theories conceive sexuality starting from the drive, not from desire. As we shall see, the difference is far from minor. Neither Mieli's theories nor the antisocial theories, in any case, are meant to inspire educational projects or anti-discrimination policies. In addition, neither one of them is adopted as an ideology by a lobby that presumably would condition government education agendas.[31] Before analysing Foucault's thought, however, we must spend a few words on the concept of desire.

The references to delirium and schizophrenia in *Towards a Gay Communism* originate from a theory of desire that could be considered as both a borderline version of Freudo-Marxism and its subversion. This is the schizoanalysis elaborated by Gilles Deleuze and Félix Guattari, and then reformulated by Guy Hocquenghem. In their two volumes of *Capitalism and Schizophrenia, Anti-Oedipus* (1972/2000) and *A Thousand Plateaus* (1980/2005), Deleuze and Guattari pay tribute to Reich, more than Marcuse, as the one who fully grasped the political problem of the relationship between desire and economy. At the same time, however, they invoke Nietzsche to reject the idea of origin, or essence, which characterises the Freudo-Marxist conception of desire.[32] Their polemic is also directed at Lacan's interpretation of Freudian theory, according to which desire would emerge as *lack* within the Oedipal triangle, following the prohibition, by the father to the son, to love the mother. In their view, Lacan ascribes to the family, the cell of bourgeois society, the status of a universal and immutable ontological structure, doomed to repeat itself from generation to generation, whereas Freud, despite all of his hesitations and contradictions, was fully aware of the revolutionary power of desire. To the developments of psychoanalysis in Freudo-Marxism and to Lacan's thought, Deleuze and Guattari oppose the idea that desire does not revolve around a structural lack in subject, but is a schizophrenic productive machine, with endless resources, which would fill the world with unpredictable contents, if capitalism did not exploit it for its own ends. Deleuze and Guattari therefore share with Freudo-Marxism both the concept of anti-capitalism and a revolutionary perspective, in addition to their insistence on the question of desire, for which, however, they elaborate a very different ontology.

The revolutionary perspective is instead absent in *Le Désir homosexuel* by Guy Hocquenghem, published in 1972 like *The Anti-Oedipus*, in which schizoanalysis is reinterpreted from the perspective of a (young) gay man living in a heterosexist society such as the French one of the early 1970s, where not only the Communist Party but even the movements of the New Left refuse to accept the demands of the homosexual liberation movement.[33] For Hocquenghem, the heterosexism of Reich is symptomatic of how both psychoanalysis and Marxism share with capitalism a symbolic order, in which desire can only be conceptualised by incorporating its productive force into a reproductive one.

This, in his opinion, is the reason why between desire and revolution 'something always seems to go wrong' (Hocquenghem, 1972/ 1993, p.135).[34] In place of the sexual revolution announced by Freudo-Marxist authors, Hocquenghem then advocates for a 'homosexual struggle' whose aim is the sexualisation of the public sphere, as opposed to the privatisation of sexuality within the family. If for Freud, as Marcuse reminds us, social relationships are sublimated homosexual relationships, for Hocquenghem the homosexual struggle is a 'wildcat' struggle that gives up any ideas of social progress to exhaust itself in the present; a struggle that does not announce 'a new stage of civilised humanity' but denounces that 'civilisation is the trap into which desire keeps falling' (p.138). Such struggle brings sex into the social field at once, in spite of the ideals of civilisation shared by bourgeoisie and working class alike as the framework of their conflicts. According to Hocquenghem, the homosexual struggle also implies a re-evaluation of the desiring function of the anus, which, in his opinion, is equivalent to the rejection not only of the specific spatiality of oedipal civilisation – that is, the distinction between public and private[35] – but also of the specific temporality of such civilisation, that is, of that 'hierarchical succession' (1972/1993, p.109) of generations in which children are subject to parents and parents sacrifice their present for a future in which children in turn will become parents. His intention, however, is not to equate homosexuality with anality. Hocquenghem too is hostile to the heterosexual model of inversion and reminds us that women too have an anus and that this latter, in men, should not be considered as a substitute for the vagina (p.103).[36] To claim the value of anal desire does not mean for him simply to praise the so-called 'passivity' of homosexual males who let themselves be penetrated, but far more ambitiously to valorise that non-reproductive, not-exclusively-genital and pre-personal form of sexuality that Freud associates with the immaturity of the child.[37]

Hocquenghem disputes the thesis of the existence of an ontological specificity of homosexuality, anticipating Foucault's thesis in *La volonté de savoir*, according to whom the concept of homosexuality was introduced into sexology only in the second half of the nineteenth century. He concludes by saying that desire is just desire, without qualifications, while homosexuality is a 'psychologically repressive category' (Hocquenghem, 1972/1993, p.51), introduced only recently. Mieli therefore has good reasons to refer to him as one of his sources, even though he then refers to Marcuse when he talks about perverse polymorphism as a form of primal desire, and not as the productive force, or machine, theorised by Deleuze and Guattari. As for Foucault – as I will now finally show – he articulates a radical critique of the concept of desire, arguing openly against the spread of Freudo-Marxism among the protest movements of the 1970s, and implicitly against the success of *Anti-Oedipus*. For him, sexuality is a dispositive of power, that is, a complex ordering structure made of linguistic, religious, moral, scientific and juridical laws, norms and conventions, which are enforced upon the subject by way of shaping their relations with others and with themselves. According to the concept of power theorised by Foucault (as an 'action exercised on actions', which I have presented in the first chapter), it is certainly possible for the subject to oppose resistance to the dispositive of sexuality. However, in order for that opposition to be effective, in his opinion, it should be based not on a hermeneutics of desire but on the pursuit of pleasure.[38]

Foucault reaches these conclusions through his critique of the repressive conceptualisation of power that he observes in Freudo-Marxism (in *La volonté de savoir* there are explicit references to Reich,[39] and in subsequent texts also to Marcuse[40]). Following Deleuze and Guattari, Foucault links this conceptualisation of power to Lacan's theorisation of desire, and also to the classical contractual theory of sovereignty. In his view, this concept is 'defined in an unusually restrictive way':

> Underlying both the general theme that power represses sex and the idea that the law constitutes desire, one encounters the same putative mechanics of power. It is defined in a strangely restrictive way, in that, to begin with, this power is poor in resources, sparing of its methods, monotonous in the tactics it utilizes, incapable of invention, and seemingly doomed always to repeat itself. Further, it is a power that only has the force of the negative on its side, a power to say no; in no condition to produce, capable only of posting limits, it is basically anti-energy. This is the paradox of its effectiveness: it is incapable of doing anything, except to render what it dominates incapable

of doing anything either, except for what this power allows it to do. And finally, it is a power whose model is essentially juridical, centered on nothing more than the statement of the law and the operation of taboos. All the modes of domination, submission, and subjugation are ultimately reduced to an effect of obedience.

(1976/1978, p.85)

Foucault's argument against Freudo-Marxism is that the main relationship between power and sexuality in modern societies is characterised not by *repression*, but by *production*. In his view, the dispositive of sexuality seeks not to abolish, but on the contrary to nourish 'perversions', understood less as behaviours, than as minority sexual *identities*, which are defined by a particular truth of desire. Just as Mieli identifies in the Judeo-Christian cultural tradition (1977/ 2018, pp.64, 96) the origin of the repression of homosexuality in the West, Foucault identifies the driving force of the 'dispositive of sexuality' in the practice of *confession*, which was spread by Catholicism across the Western world. In his opinion, people have learned to interpret their own desires by confessing the truth about their own sex in front of a priest-pastor, who throughout history has been substituted by a physician, a psychiatrist, a sexologist, a psychologist and a psychoanalyst. I have already shown (and partially thrown into question) that Foucault – anticipated by Hocquenghem – places 'the invention' of homosexuality in the second half of the nineteenth century, when sexology identified the essence of homosexual identity in a particular quality of desire: the inversion between male and female elements of the mind.

Today we cannot avoid noting that Foucault fails to reflect on the subsequent introduction of the concepts of gender and sexual orientation, and the consequent distinction between homosexuality and transsexuality. This said, the fact remains that he developed the critical methodology through which we can now think about the categories with which we currently classify sexual identities not as consequences of natural facts, but as cultural constructs endowed with a history, that is, as products of a power apparatus. It is this approach that allows Foucault to put forward – not at the level of individual psychology, but at that of social history – those hypotheses about the genesis of homosexuality that Mieli declares himself incapable of formulating. Moreover, Foucault's approach allows us to acknowledge that, in modern societies, the widespread medicalisation of society and the wide discursive production on sexuality, in which psychoanalysis also plays a part, produce not only effects of repression, or of sexual liberation, but also, and above all, the spread of a complex network of norms that control behaviours, shape identities, and even manipulate bodies. Foucault does not elaborate on the system of classification sex-gender-sexual orientation, but the critique of such system, which I carried out in the previous chapter, is a continuation of his thought. The recognition and simultaneous erasure of intersexual bodies, and the medicalisation and the construction of transsexual bodies are the result of a normative system that captures all bodies and identities, including those of cisgendered heterosexual women and men. The reason why Foucault's constructivism can be defined as 'radical' is because, according to the interpretative perspective he inaugurates, gender is not the cultural interpretation of sex, and sex is neither a biological nor psychological, or 'natural', datum. On the contrary, sex itself is the outcome of the norms of the dispositive of sexuality, in particular gender norms:

> By creating the imaginary element that is 'sex,' the deployment of sexuality established one of its most essential internal operating principles: the desire for sex—the desire to have it, to have access to it, to discover it, to liberate it, to articulate it in discourse, to formulate it in truth. It constituted 'sex' itself as something desirable. And it is this desirability of sex that attaches each one of us to the injunction to know it, to reveal its law and its power; it is this desirability that makes us think we are affirming the rights of our sex against all power, when in fact we are fastened to the deployment of sexuality that has lifted up from deep within us a sort of mirage in which we think we see ourselves reflected—the dark shimmer of sex ... So we must not refer a history of sexuality to the agency of sex; but rather show how 'sex' is historically subordinate to sexuality. We must not place sex on the side of reality, and sexuality on that of confused ideas and illusions; sexuality is a very real

historical formation; it is what gave rise to the notion of sex, as a speculative element necessary to its operation.

(Foucault, 1976/1978, pp.156–157)

Foucault has fully embodied being a philosopher in the sense given to this term by Deleuze and Guattari (that is, a friend and inventor of concepts). In the lexicon he invented, the dispositive of sexuality – which comprises personal identity, family relations, education, reproductive processes etc. – constitutes the link between the micro-physical governing of individual behaviour and the macrophysical governing of the masses; in other words, between what he calls disciplinary power (the training techniques that act on individual human beings turning them into docile bodies[41]) and what he calls biopolitics (the whole set of surveillance and regulatory procedures used upon vital processes, which transform the human species from a disorderly multitude into a manageable population[42]). The concept of politics coined by Foucault constitutes a challenge to modern political thinking. For the latter, the field of politics emerges from the premise of free and equal individuals who establish State power through a pact that binds them to obey the laws promulgated by the sovereign; Foucault, on the other hand, shows that the so-called individual is the contingent product of the joint action of multiple powers. These powers produce such individuals by following rules which are not merely laws passed by the State but are also standards of normalcy developed by the human sciences – and, before them, found in traditions, religions and in cultural and social conventions.[43] Against the philosophical anthropologies of modern thought, aimed at establishing the legitimacy of power on the basis of some essential aspects of human nature, Foucault juxtaposes his ontology of actuality, which is also an 'ontology of ourselves' – that is, an analysis not of what we have always been as humans, but of what we are now, of what we have become by virtue of the powers that have shaped us into the kind of humans that we are today.

A whole line of research in queer studies was opened up by this reversal of perspective. In the late 1990s, for example, Michael Warner suggested that in their critical evaluation of lesbian and gay movements' marriage rights demands, queer theories should not treat them exclusively as the expression of an 'individual's imitation of a model', but should take into account the 'the social, institutional, and narrative dimensions of normativity' (1999, p.154),[44] and therefore the normalising hold that an institution so loaded with history and symbolic meanings has on 'individuals' themselves. Later on, in the mid-2000s, the aforementioned Jasbir Puar introduces the category of homonationalism and asks how homosexual subjectivity, and in particular gay subjectivity, has been rewritten by the nationalist discourses developed after the events of 11 September 2001, in which the legal achievements of sexual minorities in the United States were used as a confirmation of the superiority of Western liberalism over Islamic culture (Puar, 2007). In the same period Joseph A. Massad (2007) denounces how a whole network of non-governmental organisations, agencies for the promotion of human rights and international regulations, which he calls the 'Gay International', are continuing the work of exporting the dispositive of sexuality to the Arab world, which started during the nineteenth century's colonial period, with the result of producing in the Middle East homosexual subjects that are complicit with the sexual epistemology of the West.[45] As well, Rosi Braidotti and Paul B. Preciado insist, in different ways, on the need to update concepts such as biopolitics and the dispositive of sexuality, which Foucault deploys in his analytic of power, in order to adapt them to the rapid changes of our current times. With the category of 'post-human *zoe*-politics', Braidotti describes a present in which 'advanced capitalism' governs not only the life of the human species, but the genetic code of life itself, no longer limiting itself to governing human beings understood as 'liberal individuals', but treating them as 'biogenetic "dividuals"', 'carriers of vital information' (2013, pp.117–118).[46] In turn, Preciado coins the term 'pharmacopornographic regime' to illustrate how, since the 1950s, the introduction of the distinction between gender and sexual orientation, 'the "invention" of the biochemical notion of the hormone', 'the pharmaceutical development of synthetic molecules for commercial uses' along with the spread of the contraceptive pill, the biotechnological advances, and finally the development of mass pornography amplified by the advent of the Internet, on the one hand have renewed the tools through which 'techno-capitalism' governs, exploits and capitalises on life, and on the other have 'radically modified traditional definitions of normal or pathological sexual identities' (2013, p.26).[47]

Foucault's radical constructivist methodology was also adopted by Judith Butler, whose thought has gained such resonance that it has become an unavoidable point of reference for both queer philosophers and their opponents (not only for Warner, Puar, Braidotti, Preciado and for the antisocial theorists that I will discuss in the next pages, but also for the promoters of the anti-gender campaign). In key texts such as the previously mentioned *Gender Trouble: Feminism and the Subversion of Identity* (1990), *Bodies that Matter* (1993) and *Undoing Gender* (2004a), Butler, like Mieli, supports an alliance between feminist movements and sexual minority movements, but does so by using very different arguments. She engages in a critical dialogue with feminist thought, in order to argue that, although female identity is necessary for women to constitute themselves as political subjects, feminists are likely to remain subordinate to the regime of power which subordinates women to men, unless they throw into question the enabling conditions of their self-representation as women. Drawing on Foucault's critique of modern contractualism, Butler argues that assuming the existence of the subject 'woman' – or any other subject – prior to any power relationship is a remnant of 'that foundationalist fable constitutive of the juridical structures of classical liberalism [which is the] state of nature hypothesis' (1999 [1990], p.5).[48] Still in the wake of Foucault's thought, Butler also reworks Adrienne Rich and Monique Wittig's theses, and gives the name of 'heterosexual matrix' to the normative apparatus that produces the feminine and the masculine in their asymmetrical complementarity, understood not only as sexual identities, but also as sexed bodies. Butler therefore challenges the sex-gender-sexual-orientation binary system, which postulates the existence of two distinct biological sexes, against which sexual desire is defined. On the contrary, in her interpretative perspective, it is compulsory heterosexuality that regulates gender as a binary relationship wherein the masculine becomes differentiated from the feminine through desire and its practices. Therefore, it is not the two sexes that set up the distinction between heterosexuality and homosexuality, but it is heterosexuality that defines the difference between the sexes. The heterosexual matrix, thus, discursively produces sex as a gender category and gender as a category of heterosexual desire. This is why, as I pointed out in Chapter 2, the concept of sexual orientation stops working as soon as the binary – and hence heterosexist – interpretation of sex and gender is called into question: precisely, because gender and sex themselves derive from (hetero)sexual orientation. And this is also why the sex-gender-sexual-orientation system does not allow us to account for phenomena such as gay effeminacy and lesbian masculinity. Within this system, paradoxically, the gay man is understood as a heterosexual cisgender man attracted to heterosexual men, while the lesbian as a heterosexual cisgender woman attracted to heterosexual cisgender women!

Butler therefore follows Foucault also in arguing that not only the heterosexual matrix produces subjects for whom there is 'coherence' between sex, gender, sexual desire and practices (i.e. heterosexual cisgender men and women), but also that minority sexual identities emerge from the same heterosexist dispositive, and are then penalised by it. In *Undoing Gender*, Butler examines – in ways not far from what I tried to do in Chapter 2 – the status of transgenderism and intersexuality in the contemporary biomedical paradigm.[49] At the heart of the considerations found in *Gender Trouble* and *Bodies that Matter* is, instead, the subversion of gender elaborated in those performances, common in LGBT clubs, where male actors and singers, called 'drag queens', stage an exaggerated version of femininity through gesture, hairstyles and makeup, often without completely hiding their male body under the stage costumes; or the subversion of gender elaborated by female actors and singers, called 'drag kings', who act wearing male clothes and provide a hyperbolic representation of masculinity. According to Butler, drag parody destabilises the distinctions between natural and artificial, between interior and exterior, and shows that gender – *every* gender – is not a being, but a doing, 'though not a doing by a subject who might be said to preexist the deed' (1999 [1990], p.33). It shows, in short, that gender itself is a performance, and that the 'central protagonists' of the 'naturalizing narratives of compulsory heterosexuality' (p.187), namely Man and Woman, are nothing but stylised repetitions of gestures, modelled on ideals that no real human being could ever fully embody. Unlike what is likely to happen in LGBT clubs, the register of this play in everyday life is anything but comical. Gender is a play believed to be real, in which the actors gamble with their own cultural survival. Those who do not play their role properly are exposed to the mockery and violence of others, are expelled as excrement and banished from belonging to a full humanity.[50]

The subversion performed by drag works for Butler as an example of how political action can be thought and practised by the sexual subject within a radical constructivist perspective, in which the subject does not exist prior to the norms that shape it into being. According to the Freudo-Marxist tradition, the sexual subject in capitalist society is crushed by power's repressive structures (even when their 'perversion' is exploited for profit). However, 'underneath' power's repressive structures the subject nonetheless *exists* (for Mieli, for example, this subject is formed by originary transsexuality), and the aim of the revolutionary political action is precisely to liberate it. What happens, instead, to the ability to confront power, if the subject does not exist 'prior' to power but is a consequence of it? In this case, political action is no longer conceivable in terms of a definitive revolutionary act. Foucault argues that this opposition to power takes the form of what he calls 'resistance', that is a creative oppositional action against power that modifies the same subject who undertakes it. In his view, the sexual subject's resistance against the dispositive of sexuality cannot emerge through the expression of an originary sex or desire, because the very idea of an originary sex or desire is implicated in the dispositive of sexuality. On the contrary, sexual resistance will be expressed through the elaboration of new modes of subjectivity, new provisional identities, new lifestyles, new communities, and finally through the experimentation of new practices of *pleasure* that escape the rules of normalcy:

> We must not think that by saying yes to sex, one says no to power; on the contrary, one tracks along the course laid out by the general deployment of sexuality. It is the agency of sex that we must break away from, if we aim – through a tactical reversal of the various mechanisms of sexuality – to counter the grips of power with the claims of bodies, pleasures, and knowledges, in their multiplicity and their possibility of resistance. The rallying point for the counterattack against the deployment of sexuality ought not to be sex-desire, but bodies and pleasures.
>
> (Foucault, 1978, p.157)

The emergence of transgender and intersex political subjectivity, and the very same political re-appropriation of the term 'queer' are clear examples of resistance against the contemporary dispositive of sexuality, which Foucault did not manage to witness.

In a few interviews from the early 1980s, the French philosopher instead describes the subculture that he experienced first-hand in the gay clubs of San Francisco, whose value he believes lies in its 'desexualising' of pleasure, that is, its *degenitalizing* of it – if I understand correctly the use he makes of this verb – allowing thus to extend pleasure beyond the genitals to the whole surface of the body:

> I don't think that this movement of sexual practices has anything to do with the disclosure or the uncovering of S&M tendencies deep within our unconscious, and so on. I think that S&M is much more than that; it's the real creation of new possibilities of pleasure, which people had no idea about previously. The idea that S&M is related to a deep violence, that S&M practice is a way of liberating this violence, this aggression, is stupid. We know very well what all those people are doing is not aggressive; they are inventing new possibilities of pleasure with strange parts of their body – through the eroticization of the body. I think it's a kind of creation, a creative enterprise, which has as one of its main features what I call the *desexualization* of pleasure. The idea that bodily pleasure should always come from sexual pleasure as the root of *all* our possible pleasure – I think *that*'s something quite wrong. These practices are insisting that we can produce pleasure with very odd things, very strange parts of our bodies, in very unusual situations, and so on ... The S&M ghetto in San Francisco is a good example of a community that has experimented with, and formed an identity around, pleasure ... The practice of S&M is the creation of pleasure, and there is an identity with that creation. And that's why S&M is really a subculture.
>
> (Foucault, 1997, pp.165, 167, 169–170, italics added)

Butler (2004a) as well gives evidence of what she observed in American LGBT communities when she was an undergraduate and postgraduate student at Yale University in the late 1970s and early 1980s.[51] The component of sexuality on which Butler focuses her attention is not, however, the pursuit of pleasure, but the processes of acquisition of gender identity. In drag practices, Butler (1999 [1990]) finds an example of creative resistance to gender norms that occurs through a process that she alternately calls 'subversion' and 'displacement'. As I already mentioned, Butler borrows from Foucault the idea that no subject, not even those belonging to a sexual minority, occupies a position of exteriority with respect to the heterosexual matrix (Butler, 1999 [1990]).[52] As a consequence, even the drag queen is a 'scandalously impure' creature (Butler, 2000, p.17), compromised by the normative system that she nonetheless transgresses. Again, the Foucauldian influence on Butler is visible when she argues that the drag queen doesn't express at all an original desire, her own or the one she shares with humankind,[53] and that the repression of desire is not the beginning and end of gender norms, because the very idea of the removal of an original desire is produced by such norms:

> Foucault's critique of the repressive-hypothesis in *The History of Sexuality, Volume I*, argues that (a) the structuralist 'law' might be understood as one formation of *power*, a specific historical configuration and that (b) the law might be understood to produce or generate the desire it is said to repress ... In other words, desire and its repression are an occasion for the consolidation of juridical structures; desire is manufactured and forbidden as a ritual symbolic gesture whereby the juridical model exercises and consolidates its own power.
>
> (Butler, 1999 [1990], p.96)

A definitive revolutionary suppression of gender norms is therefore not possible, nor is it possible to avoid the performative repetitions prescribed by them, which constitute us as subjects. It is possible, however, in the very repetition of these performances, to introduce deviations, variations and subversive re-appropriations of such norms so that, when these performances succeed in obtaining the acknowledgment of a public – as it happens in LGBT clubs, in queer communities and societies where LGBTQI+ movements gain visibility – they are able to change both the public and the performers. Butler uses the verb 'to displace' to indicate this complex dialectical process:

> To enter into the repetitive practices of this terrain of sig-
> nification is not a choice, for the 'I' that might enter is always
> already inside: there is no possibility of agency or reality out-
> side of the discursive practices that give those terms the intel-
> ligibility that they have. The task is not whether to repeat, but
> how to repeat or, indeed, to repeat and, through a radical pro-
> liferation of gender, *to displace* the very gender norms that
> enable the repetition itself.
>
> (Butler, 1999 [1990], p.189)

To summarise, in the radical constructivist perspective that Butler inherits from Foucault, the sexual subject has no access to any foothold outside of the dispositive of sexuality (neither desire nor sex can provide such hold) and resistance is possible only by way of leaning on the rules dictated by the dispositive itself. For example, by acting in concert, feminist and lesbian, gay, bisexual, transgender, intersex and asexual people can collectively introduce variations in the gender performances that constitute them, creating new modes of subjectivation, new styles of existence, new communities of recognition (more pleasurable, to use Foucault's lexicon; or more 'livable', to use Butler's[54]). Despite their major differences, queer constructivist theories and Freudo-Marxism therefore share an approach that isn't solely antagonistic, but also optimistic, insofar as they share a similar trust in the transformative possibilities of political action.

After the failure of the sexual liberation movements' revolutionary project in the 1970s, mainstream LGBT movements today champion the inclusion of sexual minorities in the neoliberal society as is: that is, they want full citizenship for sexual minorities within the nation State, and the extension to gays and lesbians of marriage and reproductive rights already guaranteed to heterosexual citizens. On the contrary, queer constructivist theories perform a radical critique of the present, positing the feminist lesson according to which the 'personal is political' against the distinction between public and private, typical of liberal thought. Their aim is to amplify, here and now, and immediately, the voices of new subjectivities that are socially and existentially subversive, who do not intend to be governed by the heterosexist, homo/trans-normative, homonationalist, racist and classist dispositives of the present.

3.3 Antisocial theories and affective turn

Despite being complex and counterintuitive, queer theories that follow Foucault and Butler's thought are after all reassuring in their progressivism. Such theories suggest that – although both LGBTQI + subjects and heterosexual cisgender subjects are shaped by power, and there is no original sex or desire to be liberated from 'underneath' it – for both LGBTQI+ subjects and for heterosexual cisgender subjects, there exist innumerable practices of freedom and pleasure that can be imagined and invented 'within' the very fabric of power itself. Unlike Marcuse and Mieli, Foucault and Butler do not predict the end of history by means of imagining a completely pacified society. In their view, the resistance against the dispositive of sexuality and the dislocation of those gender norms dictated by the heterosexual matrix are potentially infinite processes. Indeed, as an example, queer theorists and movements have embarked on a new season of struggles against homo/trans-normativity and homonationalism after obtaining civil rights for lesbians and gays. Hence, in addition to elaborating a radical constructivist interpretation of sexuality, Foucault and Butler assume a radically critical posture.[55] Both observe the practices of sexual dissidence of their time and participate in them. Neither one of them, however, claims that theory should have the function of planning, predicting and directing feminist movements, homosexual liberation movements and LGBTI+ movements towards a final goal. Nonetheless, it remains the case that the two philosophers welcome the possibility of building a progressively freer future – as if they had inherited from Kant an Enlightenment-style trust in the constant progress of humanity 'towards the better' (Kant, 2006, p.151).[56] These hopes contrast with the pessimistic realism of other contemporary queer theories, which, rather than advocate resistance against the dispositive of sexuality through the construction of new subjectivities and newly recognised and recognisable communities – and of more pleasurable or more livable lives – insist on the fact that the sexual drive is an irruptive force, which always provokes a rupture of the social bond and the shattering of the subject in jouissance. These are the so-called 'antisocial theories'.[57]

In the United States, Leo Bersani is usually considered the 'father' of this 'tradition'. In the now classic article 'Is the Rectum a

Grave?' he challenges Foucault with a simple but fundamental objection, stating that the French philosopher, as the majority of people, 'did not like sex' (2010, p.3).[58] 'Is the Rectum a Grave?' was first published in the magazine *October* in 1987, at the height of the AIDS crisis. Three years before Foucault himself had died from the epidemic, and in the meantime the reception of *La volonté de savoir* in American universities inaugurated an intense debate that shortly after would lead to the birth of Queer Theory. Bersani reacted against the flourishing of research and academic reflections on sexual minority subjects, on their stories and their practices, by claiming that Foucault 'did not like sex'. Why? And why does Bersani repeat the same statement in *Homos* (1995), eight years later, at a time when the success gained by Butler, who had transformed the Foucauldian analysis of the dispositive of sexuality into a critique of gender norms, was expanding the reach of the American queer debate to the whole world? Because Bersani wants to highlight that neither Foucault nor Butler, nor most of the participants in the queer constructivist theories' debate, adopt the disenchanted attitude necessary to look at sex for what it really is, in its disturbing, dysfunctional, immoral, and disgusting aspects, which both excite and provoke 'aversion':

> In saying that most people don't like sex, I'm not arguing (nor, obviously, am I denying) that the most rigidly moralistic dicta about sex hide smouldering volcanoes of repressed sexual desire. When you make this argument, you divide people into two camps, and at the same time you let it be known to which camp you belong. There are, you intimate, those who can't face their sexual desires (or, correlatively, the relation between those desires and their views of sex), and those who know that such a relation exists and who are presumably unafraid of their own sexual impulses. Rather, I'm interested in something else, something both camps have in common, which may be a certain *aversion*, an aversion that is not the same thing as a repression and that can coexist quite comfortably with, say, the most enthusiastic endorsement of polysexuality with multiple sex partners.
>
> (2010, p.4)

Bersani's (2010) critique of the queer constructivist theories and the Freudo-Marxist theories of sexual liberation[59] should therefore not be confused with an alleged complicity with traditional sexphobic moralism. On the contrary, he accuses these theories of having too hastily distanced themselves from such tradition, providing a 'positive' and 'politically correct' representation of sex, as the dimension upon which the subject's freedom depends. This critique goes beyond Foucault's objection to the theories of sexual repression, because what is called into question is not the possibility of finding the essential truth of the subject in sex, but the possibility of turning sex *as sex* into a political issue. According to Bersani, the progressive politicisation of sex is the result of the desire to cleanse sex of its own negativity, which ultimately equals the desexualisation of sex.

Truth be told, in *La volonté de savoir*, Foucault explicitly refuses to ask exactly *what* sex is. Except for a few quick final references to 'bodies' and 'pleasures' as privileged vehicles for the practice of freedom, his analysis concerns not sex, but sexuality as a biopolitical dispositive. Similarly, but also very differently, in *Gender Trouble, Bodies that Matter* and *Undoing Gender* Butler is interested in sex primarily insofar as it is made intelligible by gender. Indeed, it is gender, not sex, that is the main focus of her thinking. In both cases, whether it is the subject's *sexuality* or *gender*, each is given the task of opposing resistance – a voluntary, conscious and creative resistance to the norms that simultaneously enable and oppress that very same subject. What is at stake here, then, is, in a certain sense, the subject of progressive politics, the 'liberal subject' of Bersani's lexicon;[60] that subject – we could add[61] – modelled on the economic-rational individual theorised by Hobbes, engaged in the perennial search for their own profit, of which pleasure, livability and social recognition are basically only articulations. The reason why Foucault did not manage to distance himself from this conception of the subject lies, for Bersani, in his attempt to dismiss the use of psychoanalysis in political thought.[62] In order to clarify what a liberal interpretation of the sexual subject leaves out, and what disturbs the inscription of sex *as* sex in a political horizon, Bersani then proposes a return to Freud's *Three Essays on the Theory of Sexuality*, insisting not on the categories of perverse polymorphism and original bisexuality, which were so important for Marcuse and Mieli, but on the concept of the *drive* (*Trieb*). The subject of the drive does not pursue their own profit, neither in the form of social recognition, nor in the form of pleasure. Such a subject is not able to pursue anything, because they are rather pursued, or perhaps it would be better to say persecuted (in the sense of possessed) by the drive, which acts in them regardless of their will. Following not only Freud's theses, but also Jean Laplanche's (1970/ 1976, 1992, 2011), Bersani argues that the sexual drive is a disturbing force that dominates the subject; that makes them lose control over the world, over other people and themself; that isolates the subject from human society – for example by making them do things that they would be ashamed of doing in front of others, and for which they don't seek any recognition. The sexual drive leads the subject to a 'self-shattering' that 'disrupts the ego's coherence' dissolving its boundaries not in pleasure, but in a sexual enjoyment (*jouissance*[63]) (Bersani, 1995) that is *Beyond the Pleasure Principle* (Freud 1920/1959). In this sense, even though Freud distinguishes between the sexual drive and the death drive, for Laplanche and Bersani the sexual drive *is* death drive, and sexuality – as stated in 'Is the Rectum a Grave?' – is a tautology for masochism:

> The sexual emerges as the *jouissance* of exploded limits, as the ecstatic suffering into which the human organism momentarily plunges when it is 'pressed' beyond a certain threshold of endurance. Sexuality, at least in the mode in which it is constituted, may be a tautology for masochism.
>
> (Bersani, 2010, p.24)

The 'compulsion to rewrite sex', which according to Bersani plagues Foucault, becomes thus most evident when, in order to ignore the masochistic character of the sexual drive, he comes to represent sadomasochism as a mere pursuit of pleasure.[64] However, this compulsion is already present in the main thesis of *La volonté de savoir*, according to which sexuality can be interpreted as a dispositive of power, which can be resisted with hedonistic creativity. For Bersani, the reason why the French philosopher proposes to redeem sex through political action lies in the fact that Foucault's liberal conception of the subject is incompatible with the dysfunctional character of the sexual:

The ambition of performing sex as *only* power is a salvational project, one designed to preserve us from a nightmare of onto-logical obscenity, from the prospect of a breakdown of the human itself in sexual intensities, from a kind of selfless com-munication with 'lower' orders of being.

(Bersani, 2010, p.29)

Bersani's thought, and queer antisocial theories more in general, have in common with Freudo-Marxism the use of psychoanalysis as a phi-losophical anthropology that allows them to formulate 'universal truths' about sex. The outcome, however, is different in the two cases. For Bersani, the obscenity of the sexual is ontological, and as such it does not derive from any *History of Sexuality*, not even from that history of repression, which for Mieli begins with the Catholic religion and continues with capitalism. The drive's unsettling force is devoid of history and is present in every period and in every society. This force underlies both hetero- and homo-sexual practices. However, in het-erosexist societies, i.e. in all known societies, its negativity is projected mainly on homosexual practices, which cannot be redeemed from the reproductive purpose that can be instead attributed to the penis-vagina coitus. The central thesis of 'Is the Rectum a Grave?' is, therefore, that the outbreak of the AIDS epidemic in the 1980s literalised the threat of death, which the heterosexual imagination has always associated with homosexual sex, in particular anal sex between men. It did so by legitimising the fantasy that the sexuality of those who occupy the so-called 'passive' role in penetrative sex, is intrinsically unbridled and sick (Bersani, 2010).[65] What provokes the most dismay about a passive gay man is that, by renouncing his penetrative role as a male, he not only relinquishes a position of power, but he also bears witness to the possibility that loss of control, impotence and humiliation might be sites of enjoyment for the human. This possibility sharply contrasts with the image that the hegemonic subject – male, cisgender, hetero-sexual, able-bodied and wealthy – has been using to represent and celebrate his own self for thousands of years (and still to this day in liberal progressive thought):

Phallocentrism is exactly that: not primarily the denial of power to women (although it has obviously also led to that, everywhere and at all times), but above all the denial of the

value of powerlessness in both men and women. I don't mean
the value of gentleness, or nonaggressiveness, or even of passivity, but rather of a more radical disintegration and humiliation of the self.

(Bersani, 2010, p.24)

'Is the Rectum a Grave?', then, invites sexual minorities 'to accept
the pain of embracing, at least provisionally, a homophobic representation of homosexuality' (Bersani, 2010, p.15). In other words,
he invites them to examine thoroughly the sexual negativity that
they socially embody, before attempting to neutralise it through the
demand for a right to affectivity (civil unions and marriage) in the
hopes of being integrated *as sexual minorities* into the model of
humanity that excludes them. In later texts, such as *Homos* (Bersani, 1995) and *Intimacies* (Bersani and Phillips, 2008) – both texts
published following the introduction of AIDS' antiretroviral therapies in the mid-1990s and during a period of relentless campaigning
for civil rights in the United States, which will bring the Supreme
Court to extend marriage rights to same-sex couples in 2015 – Bersani invites again, especially gay men, to look with disenchanted
eyes at their shared lived experiences. In the compulsive consumption of pornographic material, in the gay saunas, in the cruising
bars, in the darkrooms, in BDSM and barebackers'[66] nightclubs, it
becomes evident that 'fucking has [nothing] to do with community
or love' (Bersani, 2010, p.22). The conclusion is that, if the rectum,
as the epitome of sex's negativity, is the grave of the hegemonic
subject whose civilisational ideal is built on the disgust for sex,
rather than trying to emancipate themselves from this vile organ,
queer subjects should celebrate it as the privileged locus where the
sexual drive implants itself as the death drive it is:

But if the rectum is the grave in which the masculine ideal (an
ideal shared—differently—by men *and* women) of proud subjectivity is buried, then it should be celebrated for its very
potential for death.

(Bersani, 2010, p.29)

Bersani's invitation did not fall on deaf ears. In 2009, for example,
Paul B. Preciado composed a passionate afterword to the Spanish

translation of *Le Désir homosexuel* (Preciado, 2009, 2018) – a book that Bersani does not mention either in 'Is the Rectum a Grave?' or in *Homos*, but which Preciado considers essential for a contemporary reflection on sexuality and power. For Preciado this book should be considered not only an 'instruction manual for operating an anti-system orifice installed in every and each body: the ANUS' (Preciado, 2018, p.39), but also 'a first example of a form of knowledge which is today known as queer theory' (p.41, translated by M. Baldo and E. Basile).[67] The afterword's title is 'Anal Terror', and it praises what, using a Roland Barthes expression, Preciado calls Hocquenghem's 'textual terrorism'.[68]

Both Hocquenghem and Bersani are also key reference figures for Lee Edelman, author in 2004 of *No Future: Queer Theory and the Death Drive*, a book that has opened a debate in the United States on the 'antisocial thesis in queer theory' in which Teresa de Lauretis and Jack Halberstam have taken part, among others.[69] While Bersani uses Jean Laplanche's psychoanalysis to remind sexual minorities of what they represent in the eyes of the rest of society, and to invite gay people to embrace a politically *in*correct idea of homosexuality, Edelman goes further. He makes use of Jacques Lacan's psychoanalysis to encourage queer subjects to become active representatives of the death drive, to invite them to become ruthless bards of inhumanity, prophets of the end of civilisation. Edelman's (2004) polemic against the future coincides in fact with a polemic against 'the Child', a symbol or better a fetish of the future, around which all meaning is built. Against the promise of futurity embodied by the Child, the author posits the senselessness and sterility of a *jouissance* in which the ego is engulfed by 'the real',[70] reminding readers that – rare exceptions aside – one does not fuck for reproduction, but for pleasure:

> 'A family is created' ... the phrase strategically elides the agency by which this end is achieved. No fucking could ever effect such creation: all sensory experience, all pleasure of the flesh, must be borne away from this fantasy of futurity secured, eternity's plan fulfilled, as 'a new generation is carried forward.' Paradoxically, the child of the two-parent family thus proves that its parents *don't* fuck and on its tiny shoulders it carries the burden of maintaining the fantasy of a time to come

in which meaning, at last made present to itself, no longer depends on the fantasy of its *attainment* in time to come.

(2004, p.41)

Edelman (2004) points out, for example, that in those conservative discourses well exemplified by the campaign against 'gender ideology', children are frequently invoked against homosexuals. And this is not only because sex between two women or between two men is non-reproductive, but also because homosexual couples would not be able to raise children for several reasons: (1) because children would need parental figures of opposite genders; (2) because, again, homosexuals, especially males, considered as seductive demons hungry for fresh meat, would be a threat to children; (3) and finally because simply mentioning homosexuality in schools would be a danger to their young minds, an example of *bad education*. [71]

To respond to these discourses, in which homosexuality is presented as a perverse and threatening force for the reproductive family and childhood (and 'gender ideology' is presented as the ideological argument that supports this very force), instead of pursuing their own social inclusion by claiming access to marriage, adoption, or assisted reproduction techniques, queer subjects, according to Edelman, should radically reject heterosexual sociality's values and proudly pronounce 'the words for which we're condemned' (2004, p.31):

> The queerness we propose, in Hocquenghem's words, 'is unaware of the passing of generations as stages on the road to better living. It knows nothing about "sacrifice now for the sake of future generations" ... [it] knows that civilization alone is mortal.' Even more: it delights in that mortality as the negation of everything that would define itself, moralistically, as pro-life. It is we who must bury the subject in the tomb-like hollow of the signifier, pronouncing at last the words for which we're condemned should we speak them or not: that we are the advocates of abortion; that the Child as futurity's emblem must die; that the future is mere repetition and just as lethal as the past.

(2004, p.31)

Against the modern individual, perpetually trapped in a projective imaginary that demands them to sacrifice the present for a future of which the reproductive family is both symbol and instrument, Edelman thus juxtaposes a queer subject whose sexual drive forces them to a radical adherence to the present of jouissance. Against all movements of emancipation and sexual liberation, Edelman insists on a static refusal of sociality. In so doing, he takes to the extreme Bersani's earlier critique of Foucault and Butler's constructivism.

To the Freudo-Marxist hope in an end of history where the subject can be definitively liberated through sexual revolution, Foucault and Butler counter that freedom is an endless practice, and that the power that structures sexuality cannot be abolished. They suggest, however, that this power can be subverted and dislocated through a constant reinvention of the sexual subject and a constant resignification of their social relationships. Alongside Bersani, Edelman instead argues that the sexual drive deprives the subject of freedom, isolates them from the community, leads them to dissolution in a jouissance that unsettles consciousness and leaves no room for the search for meaning. Therefore, just like the revolutionary ideal and the demand for rights, the constructivist trust in the progressive creativity of queer subjects won't save them from the disgust aroused by the negativity they represent. Edelman, I believe, wants to go beyond Bersani in his paradoxical attempt to make the sexual subject not only a subject that defies liberal political thought, but also a political subject *in their own way*. Against an idea of politics traditionally understood as the projection of a collectivity into the future and as the construction of meaning, the subject of the drive opposes their present abjection, the senseless refusal of their 'no'. From this observation, Edelman seems at times to suggest an invitation for queer subjects to abandon political action; at other times he seems to be inviting them to rethink the foundations of political action altogether.

What is certain is that the subsumption of the sexual question in the political sphere has never been either easy or obvious. In the 1970s, both Hocquenghem and Mieli confronted the reluctance of youth protest movements to accommodate the demands of sexual minorities. In the 1980s and 1990s, Bersani witnessed the setbacks suffered by hopeful gay movements as a result of the public reaction to the AIDS crisis. At the beginning of the new millennium, faced with the conservative pushback against the achievements of feminist and LGBTQI+ movements, Edelman, with a realistic attitude, argues that the *queerness* of queer subjects, the negativity that makes them such, cannot be definitively redeemed by politics, and therefore a properly queer politics cannot coincide with the pursuit of this impossible redemption. From the only standpoint we are given to occupy – and that is the present of a world wherein reactionary campaigns have taken hold in places where sexual minorities have nonetheless gained social recognition – it is indeed plausible to imagine that, even if all the States in the world were to approve marriage for gays and lesbians, many people would still feel disgust for their sexual practices; indeed, even if all the States in the world were to approve inclusive education projects in schools, homo-bi-trans-phobic bullying would still persist in schools, and in society as a whole. If Bersani invites us to take into account what he presents as the irreducible negativity of the sexual, Edelman invites us to become accountable to it. Not all contemporary queer theorists, obviously, share his position. The reflections inaugurated by Lisa Duggan and Jasbir Puar on homonormativity and homonationalism,[72] although they rarely use a psychoanalytic vocabulary and often adopt a constructivist methodology, seem to confirm, however, Edelman's vision of the political ontology of the sexual, when they denounce how the assimilation, in neoliberal societies, of some privileged subjects belonging to sexual minorities (mostly male, cisgender, white, Christian, wealthy and not-disabled ...) happens at the expense of other subjects (women, intersex, transgender, racialised, Islamic, poor, disabled ...). It is as if the negativity of the sexual can't be extinguished, but only partially and delusively projected upon others, in a zero-sum game. Moreover, those subjects who are assimilated, are so on the basis of being docile productive and reproductive citizens, husbands and fathers, wives and mothers who contribute to the future of the nation, simultaneously as agents and as objects of an investment in futurity. Not as queer subjects consumed by jouissance.

There is another strand of contemporary queer research that can also be read in continuity with antisocial theories. 'Queer Bonds'[73] was the evocative title chosen for a conference held in February 2009 at the University of California, Berkeley, which aimed at taking stock of the debate generated by antisocial theories. The expression 'affective turn' took hold in the wake of the conference, and it is now used to describe studies that examine the specificity of sexual minority subjects' relationships and affects, in an attempt to build 'affective archives' capable of restoring attention to the lived experience of queer subjects.[74] Despite the fact that reference to notions such as 'bonds' and 'affects' obviously evokes markedly different scenarios from a-sociality, these studies seem to suggest that queer relationships can only occur in the interstices of the heterosexual social order, wherein each time they provoke a rupture. Rather than overcoming antisocial theories, these studies on affect, as well as those on homonormativity and homonationalism, also demonstrate the insufficiency of the schematic distinction hitherto proposed between revolutionary Freudo-Marxism, radical constructivism, and antisocial theories. In the contemporary debate, far from being considered distinct and opposed argumentative paradigms, these often become articulations within a single line of thought, giving rise to new theoretical configurations. In response to Foucault's critique of the political use of psychoanalysis, Bersani and Edelman propose a return to Freud via Laplanche and Lacan. De Lauretis's last work, instead, puts Freud, Foucault and Fanon in dialogue with one another (de Lauretis, 2008), while Duggan and Puar use Foucault's analytics of power for a critique of neoliberalism, which resonates with Marxist ideas. In studies on queer affects, references to all these authors intersect to become part of a multidimensional analysis of the effects that neoliberal governmentality has not only on the material, but also the affective life of queer subjects (which is also material, by the way). Jack Halberstam, for example, situating his thought within the antisocial theories camp, recalls that Bersani's work 'has also been useful for the theorization of femme receptivities, butch abjection and lesbian loneliness' (Halberstam, 2006, p.823),[75] and in the articles included in the book *The Queer Art of Failure* (Halberstam, 2011) he[76] explores queer lives' sense of failure, not to claim their future 'redemption' in a more just society – which is rather what Butler tried to do – but to show the feasibility of modes of being that already escape the success imperatives of contemporary societies. In *Depression: A Public Feeling* Ann Cvetkovich (2012) similarly examines depression, that affect which the symptoms of our present condition are increasingly traced back to. Following Alain Ehrenberg (1998), Cvetkovich understands depression not as an individual pathology, but as a dispositive of power that acts micro-physically in the psycho-social fabric of our society. Insofar as it constitutes the existential fallout of a neoliberal biopolitics that does not impose rigid disciplinary codes, but demands free initiative, creativity and sense of responsibility, depression indeed punishes people who fail to contribute successfully to the future of an increasingly competitive society – and this often happens to queer subjects who do not conform to homo/trans-normative standards – making them feel 'small, worthless, hopeless' (Cvetkovich, 2012, p.13).

This insistence on angry and sad 'passions' on the part of antisocial theories and queer affective archives, can be contrasted with the feminist, Spinozist and Deleuzean enthusiasm of the already mentioned Rosi Braidotti, who in *The Posthuman* (2013) celebrates the existing one as 'simply the best of all possible posthuman worlds' (p.197), the outcome of all of our 'joint efforts and collective imaginings' (p.197). Also authors directly involved in the US queer debate, such as José Esteban Muñoz (2006, 2009), Tim Dean (2009) and Michael D. Sneadiker (2009), refuse to equate queerness with the negativity of the drive, and counter Edelman's pessimism with a reappraisal of hope, utopianism and even optimism.[77] In this case, however, as Cvetkovich points out, the distance from antisocial theories is qualified:

> Discussions of utopia and other related concepts have been part of queer theory debates about the 'antisocial,' which have circulated most prominently in connection with Lee Edelman's rejection of futurity as reproductive heteronormativity. Central to this discussion has been the question of whether it is possible to sustain a commitment to the utopian without falling into the pastoralizing or romanticizing tendencies that Edelman (echoing Leo Bersani) critiques. It should be noted, though, that queer work on the utopian generally embraces negativity, finding the utopian in perversion, abjection, failure, depression, and struggle, and hence refusing easy or binary distinctions between positive and negative affects.
>
> (2012, pp.190–191)

In short, far from being settled along rigid 'ideological' positions, the debate around the relationship between sexuality and power remains open. Furthermore, as Halberstam (2005) suggests, such openness does not respect a linear (*straight*) kind of temporality directly oriented towards the future, but works from within a crooked and weird (and *frocia* or *queer*[78]) temporality in which interruptions, bendings and overlaps alternate with returns, and a utopian and optimistic waiting can paradoxically coincide with a depressive realisation of failure (so that the positive can paradoxically coincide with the negative). Faced with this subversion of logic, it would make little sense for us to risk making predictions about the future of queer theories. What I feel I can positively say, in conclusion, is that if Freudo-Marxism, constructivism, antisocial theories and affective archives will continue to emerge and re-emerge, and if their paths will cross again forming new configurations or leaving room for something else, can only depend on the urgencies of a critique of the present.

Notes

1 For an explanation of these Italian expressions, see note 1 in Chapter 2.
2 See, for example, the public statement by the Italian Psychological Association (downloadable at www.aipass.org/files/AIP_position_sta tement_diffusione_studi_di_genere_12_marzo_2015(1).pdf) and Michela Marzano, *Papà, mamma e gender* (2015).
3 The concept of heteronormativity was introduced by Michael Warner in the preface to his edited book *Fear of a Queer Planet: Queer Politics and Social Theory* (1993). Commenting on the contributions included in the book, he states: 'In each case the authors do not simply call for the inclusion of lesbians and gays into a theory that would remain otherwise unaltered. They suggest, indeed, that the theoretical languages in question can specify sexual identities only in ways that produce the ideology of heterosexual society. Even when coupled with a toleration of minority sexualities, *heteronormativity* can be overcome only by actively imagining a necessarily and desirably queer world' (pp.xv–xvi, italics added).
4 On these topics see Muñoz (1999), Duggan (2004) and Stryker (2008).
5 Concerning the situation in the United States, in an interview in 2014 Susan Stryker stated: 'What is truly amazing to me, after having been out as trans for nearly a quarter century, is the extent to which it is now becoming possible for some trans people to access what I call "transnormative citizenship", while at the same time truly horrific life circumstances persist for other trans people. Race really does seem to be the dividing line that allows some trans people to be cultivated for life, invested in, recognized, and enfolded into the biopolitical state, while

allowing others to be consigned to malignant neglect or lethal violence'
(Stryker and Dierkes-Thrun, 2014). As far as the Italian transgender
community is concerned, see the interesting debates in Arietti et al.
(2010). On the problem of finding work for transgender people in Italy,
see instead: Oliverio et al. (2016).

6 The website of the Italian Union for the Klinefelter Syndrome (www.
unitask.it), for example, reassures: 'There is no evidence that XXY
males are more prone to homosexuality than other men. The only
relevant sexual difference between young XXY males and other youth
of the same age consists in a more moderate libido (XXY males may
have less interest in sex). However, continuous testosterone injections
can lead to standard levels of libido.' The website of the Italian Association for Androgen Insensitivity Syndrome (www.sindromedimorris.
org), on the other hand, acknowledges that androgen insensitivity syndrome is 'a form of intersex in that there is a mismatch between genetic
sex and the formation of the external genitals'. At the same time,
however, it points out that 'this condition … is different from transsexuality'. The website states: 'The people affected by this syndrome
when considered from the anatomical, psychological, legal and social
point of view, are women.' Finally, it adds that 'These women are
therefore struggling with the sorrow of not being able to have children'.
According to the two associations, in conclusion, it is important to
distinguish the two conditions from homosexuality and transsexuality
respectively, and to portray people with Klinefelter syndrome as heterosexual cisgender males who, with testosterone therapy, can reach a
higher level of sexual desire typical of 'standard men', and to portray
people with androgen insensitivity syndrome as cisgender heterosexual
women desirous of motherhood and a family.

7 Jasbir Puar (2007) speaks about homonationalist 'assemblages' to
account for the contradictory character of these discourses by borrowing the concept of 'assemblage' from Deleuze and Guattari (1980/2005).
It should be noted that, while gay rights on the one hand are opposed to
Islamic homophobia, on the other hand the press often attributes
homosexual tendencies to those responsible for Islamist terrorist
attacks, using them as signs of poor adherence to the Islamic religion,
and at the same time as symptoms of a disturbed personality. This
happened, for example, in relation to Abdeslam Salah (member of the
command responsible for the Paris attack of 13 November 2015), Omar
Marteen (author of the attack on the gay club Pulse in Orlando on 12
June 2016) and Mohamed Bouhlel (responsible for the Nice attack on
14 July 2016).

8 In relation to black queer studies see the anthology by Johnson and
Henderson (2005). See also Muñoz (1999, 2009), Ferguson (2003),
Sharpe (2010), Rifkin (2011) and Shah (2012).

9 A telling example is the following: 'I have never been able, without
revulsion, to hear a *man* say of another man: "He is so sensual!" I do

not know what the sensuality of a man is. Imagine a woman saying of another woman: "She's so terribly desirable—she's darling"' (Fanon, 1952/2008, p.156). Fanon argues that among the black people of the Antilles, whose psychology is profoundly marked by colonial domination, the Oedipus complex does not exist and therefore homosexuality does not exist. He also argues that racism is an expression of the unconscious desire, not only by white women but also by white men, to be raped by black men.

10 A remarkable example of this is the reconstruction of the situation in the UK that Simon Watney does in his article 'The Spectacle of Aids' where one can read: 'Thus in England recently *The Guardian* noted that "by the end 1,013 cases had been reported, of whom 572 had died", while the *The Star* informed *its* readers that "AIDS has now killed more than 1,000 people in Britain." Misreporting on such a scale has been regular and systematic since the earliest days of the epidemic, and is indicative of the values and priorities of an international information industry that continues to oscillate daily between meretricious gloating over the fate of those deemed responsible for their own misfortune, and the supposed "threat" of a "real" epidemic. Currently in the United States, someone dies of AIDS every half hour. An estimated six percent of all Africans have been infected by HIV, including nearly a quarter of the entire populations of Malawi and Uganda. If statistics teach us anything, it is the sheer scale and efficiency of the cultural censorship within and between different countries and continents, which guarantees that the actual situation of the vast majority of people with HIV and/or AIDS is rarely if ever discussed. Moreover, this disappearance is strategic, and faithfully duplicates the positions the social groups most vulnerable to HIV found themselves in even before the epidemic began. *Thus the Latino population of the two continents of America, IV drug users, workers in the sex industry, black Africans, and gay men are carefully confined in the penal category of the "high-risk group," from which position their experience and achievements may be safely ignored.* In this manner a terrible ongoing human catastrophe has been ruthlessly denied the status of tragedy, or even natural disaster' (Watney, 1987, p.72, italics added).

11 I refer here, in particular, to the 'Mattachine Society', a male homosexual cultural association founded in Los Angeles in 1951, and the 'Daughters of Bilitis', a female homosexual cultural association founded in 1955 in San Francisco.

12 In the already quoted article 'Transgender History, Homonormativity, and Disciplinarity' (2008), Susan Stryker reconstructs the history of a similar revolt against the police, which took place three years before the events of Stonewall, at Gene Compton's cafeteria in San Francisco, which the author defines as a club of 'drag queens, hustlers … buzzing with its usual late night crowd' (p.64).

13 The Queer Nation Manifesto can be accessed at the following link: www.historyisaweapon.com/defcon1/queernation.html.

14 I am thinking in particular of collectives, groups and networks such as 'antagonismo gay', 'Facciamo Breccia', 'laboratorio smaschieramenti', 'Favolosa Coalizione', 'SomMovimentonazioAnale', 'AH! SqueerTo! - Assemblea Queer Torino', which have recently come to define themselves as 'trans-feminists and queer' or 'puta-lesbo-trans-femministi-queer' ['slut-lesbo-trans-feminist-queer'] movements. These movements are also hotbeds of activist ideas. See, for examples, the contributions included in the book *Il genere. Tra neoliberismo e neofondamentalismo* (Zappino, 2016).

15 Translators' note: For the difference between Queer Theory and queer theories see note 32, Chapter 2 (translators' note).

16 Sexual minorities are turned into political minorities through the way in which the relationship between power and sexuality is articulated in the present. See note 22 of Chapter 1.

17 Marcuse (1955), for example, speaks of 'surplus-repression' based on a 'performance principle' that would inform all human relationships in capitalist societies, by turning work into an end in itself.

18 Reich (1936/1974) states that '1. Homosexuality is not a social crime; it harms no one. 2. It can be *restricted* only by restoring all the prerequisites for a *natural* love life among the masses. 3. Until this goal is realized, it must be considered on equal terms with heterosexual forms of gratification and should not be punished (except for the seduction of minors)' (p.221, italics added).

19 Marcuse (1955) states: 'Originally, the sex instinct has no extraneous temporal and spatial limitations on its subject and object; sexuality is by nature "polymorphous-perverse". The societal organization of the sex instinct taboos as *perversions* practically all its manifestations which do not serve or prepare for the procreative function' (p.49).

20 Mieli was among the founders of FUORI! (Fronte Unitario Omosessuale Italiano [Unitarian Homosexual Revolutionary Italian Front]) in the spring of 1971. When FUORI! joined the Radical Party in autumn 1971, Mieli did not approve of the decision and went on to found COM (Comitato Omosessuali Milanesi [Milanese Homosexual Committee]). In the 1980s he abandoned the revolutionary left and embraced pacifist and anti-nuclear positions. For further reading on the history of Italian LGBT movements until the mid-1980s see Prearo (2015).

21 Please refer to section 2.3 of Chapter 2.

22 From a certain perspective, also Feinberg's thought could be traced back to Freudo-Marxism. In fact, despite not conceiving of transgenderism, unlike Mieli, as an originary and universal condition, Feinberg still posits it as a 'natural' condition, very much like Mieli does. In their view, transgender people have always existed in the history of humanity, and if in modern societies they have been denied the right to exist, this has been mainly due to the productive and reproductive needs of capitalism. Only a communist

revolution can thus free them, and with them all human beings, from the economic system that oppresses them. See Feinberg (1992, 1997).

23 See Quaranta (2004).

24 Mieli (1977/2018) states: 'To those who still wonder whether they are born homosexual or become so, we must reply that everyone is born endowed with a wide range of erotic propensity, directed first of all towards the self and the mother, then gradually turning outward to "everyone" else, irrespective of their sex, and in fact towards the entire world. They become either heterosexual or homosexual only as a result of educastration (repressing their homoerotic impulses in the first case, and their heterosexual ones in the second)' (p.5).

25 For Mieli (1977/2018): 'Social oppression ... tends to reduce the original polymorphous richness of Eros (transsexuality) to a rigid hetero-sexuality. But why some individuals still become gay, despite the very strong condemnation of homosexual tendencies, is something that we do not as yet understand' (p.42).

26 'Homosexuality is a relation between persons of the same sex. Between women, it proclaims the autonomous existence of female sexuality, independent of the phallus. Between men, even though historically marked by phallocracy, homosexuality multiplies the sexual "unique-ness" of the phallus, thus in a certain respect negating it, and discloses the availability of the ass for intercourse and erotic pleasure' (Mieli, 1977/2018, p.245).

27 This aspect is particularly stressed by Renato Busarello (2016).

28 Wittig thus predict the extinction of Man and Woman which, in her opinion, like Race, are nothing but political classes, the result of the exploitation of the latter by the former: 'they are seen as *black*, there-fore they *are* black; they are seen as *women*, therefore they *are* women. But before being *seen* that way, they first had to be *made* that way' (1992, p.12).

29 'We revolutionary queers see in the child not so much Oedipus, or the future Oedipus, as *the potentially free human being*. We do indeed love children. We are able to desire them erotically, in response to their own erotic wishes, and we can openly and with open arms grasp the rush of sensuality that they pour out and make love with them. That is why paedophilia is so strictly condemned. It sends messages of love to the child, whom society, through the family, seeks to traumatise, educa-strate, and negate, imposing on the child's eroticism the Oedipal grid. The oppressive heterosexual society forces the child into a period of latency; but this is nothing but the deadly introduction to the prison of a latent "life". Paedophilia, on the other hand, "is an arrow of libido directed at the foetus" (Francesco Ascoli)' (Mieli, 1977/2018, p.54).

30 'The ego and the illusion of "normal reality" are the result of the indivi-dualistic atomisation of the species, an atomisation that followed and replaced the gradually destroyed community. So-called "delusion" is therefore a "state of grace", since in the individual affected the desire for

community reawakens and seeks to assert itself in surroundings which are hostile to it and [are] in fact its negation' (Mieli, 1977/2018, p.195).

31 The thesis of the existence of a 'gay' lobby or 'homosexual lobby' capable of putting pressure on national governments and European and international institutions is one of the anti-gender campaign's rallying points.

32 As Deleuze and Guattari state: 'Reich was the first to raise the problem of the relationship between desire and the social field (and went further than Marcuse, who treats the problem lightly). He is the true founder of a materialist psychiatry ... Reich, in the name of desire, caused a song of life to pass into psychoanalysis' (1972/2000, pp.118–119).

33 In 1968, Hocquenghem took part in the occupation of the Sorbonne, during which a Comité d'Action Pédérastique Révolutionnaire was established, whose banners were, however, taken away by other students. Subsequently he took part in the activities of FHAR (Front Homosexuel d'Action Révolutionnaire), founded, like the FUORI! by Mieli (see Chapter 3, note 20), in the spring of 1971. On 5 and 6 April 1972, in Sanremo, the two groups organised a protest against an international sexology conference on the *Deviant Behaviour of Human Sexuality*. The 'flickiâtres' (psycho-cops), that is, the holders of psychological knowledge about homosexuality, would also become the most frequent targets of the FHAR protests. These protests did not spare the leftist 'hétéro-flics' (heterocops). In February 1972, for example, the FHAR stormed into a conference of the French Communist Party, which tackled women's issues from a familist perspective, which members of the group considered reactionary. See FHAR (1971). On the history of French LGBT movements see Prearo (2014). And finally, on the life and thought of Hocquenghem see Marshall (1997) and Idier (2007).

34 'Something always seems to go wrong somewhere between desire and revolution ... We must give up the dream of reconciling the official spokesmen of revolution to the expression of desire. We cannot force desire to identify with a revolution which is already so heavy with the past history of the "workers" movement' (Hocquenghem, 1972/1993, p.135).

35 According to the theory of psychosexual development elaborated by Freud (1905/2017) in *Three Essays on The Theory of Sexuality*, only during the anal phase does the child grasp the rules governing spatial differentiation in civil society, by learning that defecating must be relegated to the sphere of intimacy.

36 'The problem here is not one of activity or passivity (which, according to Freud, become differentiated precisely at the anal stage) ... The anus is not a substitute for the vagina: women have one as well as men. The phallus's signifying-discerning function is established at the very same moment that the anus-organ breaks away from its imposed privatisation, in order to take part in the desire race. To reinvest the anus collectively and libidinally would involve a proportional weakening of the

great phallic signifier, which dominates us constantly both in the small-scale hierarchies of the family and in the great social hierarchies. The least acceptable desiring operation (precisely because it is the most desublimating one) is that which is directed at the anus' (Hocquenghem 1972/1993, p.103).

37 Hocquenghem's polemic against the psychoanalytic conception of 'anal desire' and against Reich's heterosexism shares some interesting similarities with Carla Lonzi's thought. In the same years in Italy, Lonzi denounced how psychoanalysis and Freudo-Marxism perpetuated the subordination of women to men by prescribing women's orgasmic achievement only through heterosexual coitus, and by accusing of immaturity those women who seek orgasm through the direct stimulation of the clitoris: 'The confusion caused by Reich's theories lies in the fact that we find in him both a new consciousness of the function of pleasure and orgasm ... and a categorically procreative vision of sexuality, which includes a patriarchal rejection of the clitoris. In the Reichian cosmogony there is no place for the only organ dedicated purely and exclusively to pleasure' (Lonzi, 1971/2013, p.95, translated by M. Baldo and E. Basile).

38 'But the problem I have is that I'm not sure if, through this very word, despite its different meaning, we don't run the risk, despite Deleuze and Guattari's intention, of allowing some of the medico-psychological presuppositions [*prises*] that were built into desire, in its traditional sense, to be reintroduced. And so it seems to me that, by using the word *pleasure*, which in the end means nothing, which is still, it seems to me, rather empty of content and unsullied by possible uses – in treating pleasure ultimately as nothing other than an event, an event that happens, that happens, I would say, outside the subject, or at the limit of the subject, or between two subjects, in this something that is neither of the body nor of the soul, neither outside nor inside – don't we have here, in trying to reflect a bit on this notion of pleasure, a means of avoiding the entire psychological and medical armature that was built into the traditional notion of desire?' (Foucault, 2011, pp.389–390).

39 'Thus between the two world wars there was formed, around Reich, the historico-political critique of sexual repression. The importance of this critique and its impact on reality were substantial. But the very possibility of its success was tied to the fact that it always unfolded within the deployment of sexuality, and not outside or against it' (Foucault, 1976/1978, p.131).

40 Marcuse, is, for example, explicitly connected to Freud and Reich in Foucault's (1978) conference paper 'Sexuality and Power' (p.128).

41 Foucault analyses the functioning of disciplinary power especially in *Discipline and Punish* (1975/1995), in his lectures from 1974, *Psychiatric Power* (2006), and in the ones from 1975, *Abnormal* (2003a).

42 Foucault develops the concept of biopolitics mainly in the last chapter of *The History of Sexuality Volume I: An Introduction* (1976/1978), in

the last lecture of his 1976 course, *Society Must Be Defended* (2003b), and in two other courses, one held in 1978, *Security, Territory, Population* (2009), and one in 1979, *The Birth of Biopolitics* (2008).

43 In *Society Must Be Defended* Foucault sums up his research programme with these words: 'The manufacture of subjects rather than the genesis of the sovereign: that is our general theme' (2003b, p.46).

44 Further on in the article Warner writes: 'In short, no theory that takes queerness as inevitable in principle, or normalization as impossible in principle, can be of much use in making the world-historical judgment of the politics of gay marriage. Perhaps the theory was not intended for that purpose. But if such theoretical arguments lull queer theorists into a false optimism about the ability of queers to resignify marriage, then it will have failed the aspiration to resist normalization. Where does this leave us? Not at the altar, to be sure' (Warner, 1999, p.157).

45 The gay international is driven, according to Massad (2007), by the attempt to 'save' Arab subjects belonging to sexual minorities from their 'backward' societies. However, for such an attempt to be possible, it pre-emptively moulds these subjects according to the identity standards of 'modern' Western homosexuality. For a critique of Massad that takes into account the possibility of an activism by 'Third World' sexual minorities not subaltern to 'homocapitalism', see Rao (2010).

46 For a critical review of Braidotti's book (2013), which in my opinion runs the risk of an unconscious heterosexism, see Bernini (2016).

47 See also Preciado (2014). An update of Foucault's analysis through the categories of 'biocapital' and 'biowork' is also found in Cooper (2008) and Cooper and Waldby (2014).

48 These words can be read as an answer to Monique Wittig who, in 1987 conference entitled 'On the Social Contract' contained in *The Straight Mind and Other Essays* (1992), argues that the modern social order is regulated by an implicit *sexual contract* that imposes gender binarism and compulsory heterosexuality. They could also be an answer to Carole Pateman, who a year later, in *The Sexual Contract* (1988) shows through careful textual analysis that in the major political works by Hobbes, Locke, Rousseau and Kant, the individuals who enter into the pact that establishes political society are men, who are owners. As a consequence of this, she argues, modernity's foundational social contract presupposes a prior sexual contract between men meant to regulate the possession of women.

49 See the chapter 'Doing Justice to Someone: Sex Reassignment and Allegories of Transsexuality', in Butler (2004a).

50 'The repudiation of bodies for their sex, sexuality, and/or color is an "expulsion" followed by a "repulsion" that founds and consolidates culturally hegemonic identities along sex/race/sexuality axes of differentiation … The boundary between the inner and outer is confounded by those excremental passages in which the inner effectively becomes outer, and this excreting function becomes, as it were, the model by

which other forms of identity-differentiation are accomplished. In effect, this is the mode by which Others become shit' (Butler, 1999 [1990], p.170). Butler here is commenting on Kristeva's text, *Powers of Horror: An Essay on Abjection* (1982) and on Young (1990).

51 'Why drag? Well, there are biographical reasons, and you might as well know that in the United States the only way to describe me in my younger years was as a bar dyke who spent her days reading Hegel and her evenings, well, at the gay bar, which occasionally became a drag bar. And I had some relatives who were, as it were, in the life, and there was some important identification with those "boys." So I was there, undergoing a cultural moment in the midst of a social and political struggle. But I also experienced in that moment a certain implicit theorization of gender: it quickly dawned on me that some of these so-called men could do femininity much better than I ever could, ever wanted to, ever would. And so I was confronted by what can only be called the transferability of the attribute. Femininity, which I understood never to have belonged to me anyway, was clearly belonging elsewhere, and I was happier to be the audience to it, have always been very happier [*sic*] to be its audience than I ever was or would be being the embodiment of it. (This does not mean, by the way, that I am therefore disembodied, as some rather mean-spirited critics have said or implied.)' (Butler, 2004a, p.213).

52 'The effort to locate and describe a sexuality "before the law" as a primary bisexuality or as an ideal and unconstrained polymorphousness implies that the law is antecedent to sexuality. As a restriction of an originary fullness, the law prohibits some set of prepunitive sexual possibilities and the sanctioning of others. But if we apply the Foucaultian critique of the repressive hypothesis to the incest taboo, that paradigmatic law of repression, then it would appear that the law produces *both* sanctioned heterosexuality and transgressive homosexuality. Both are indeed *effects*, temporally and ontologically later than the law itself, and the illusion of a sexuality before the law is itself the creation of that law' (Butler, 1999 [1990], p.94).

53 This desire would be comparable to the perverse polymorphic transsexuality discussed by Mieli.

54 For more on the concept of 'livability', by Butler, see *Bodies that Matter: On the Discursive Limits of Sex* (1993), *Antigone's Claim* (2000), *Undoing Gender* (2004a), *Giving an Account of Oneself: A Critique of Ethical Violence* (2003), *Precarious Life: The Powers of Mourning and Violence* (2004b), *Frames of War: When Is Life Grievable?* (2009) and, finally, *Notes Toward a Performative Theory of Assembly* (2015). On Butler's thought I would also like to suggest my essay, 'Riconoscersi umani nel vuoto di Dio. Judith Butler, tra Antigone ed Hegel' (Bernini, 2009).

55 On the declared 'normativism' of Butler's recent thought, see Chapter 1, note 19.

56 See Kant (2006).

57 'The Antisocial Thesis in Queer Theory' is the title of a conference held in Washington DC on 27 December 2005. Excerpts of the presentations were published in Caserio et al. (2006).

58 'Is the Rectum a Grave?' starts as follows: 'There is a big secret about sex: most people don't like it. I don't have any statistics to back this up, and I doubt (although since Kinsey there has been no shortage of polls on sexual behavior) that any poll has ever been taken in which those polled were simply asked, "Do you like sex?" Nor am I suggesting the need for any such poll, since people would probably answer the question as if they were being asked, "Do you often feel the need to have sex?" and one of my aims will be to suggest why these are two wholly different questions' (Bersani, 2010, p.3).

59 'Much of this derives of course from the rhetoric of sexual liberation in the '60s and '70s, a rhetoric that received its most prestigious intellectual justification from Foucault's call—especially in the first volume of his *History of Sexuality*—for a reinventing of the body as a surface of multiple sources of pleasure. Such calls, for all their redemptive appeal, are, however, unnecessarily and even dangerously tame. The argument for diversity has the strategic advantage of making gays seem like passionate defenders of one of the primary values of mainstream liberal culture, but to make that argument is, it seems to me, to be disingenuous about the relation between homosexual behavior and the revulsion it inspires. The revulsion, it turns out, is all a big mistake: what we're really up to is pluralism and diversity, and getting buggered is just one moment in the practice of those laudable humanistic virtues. Foucault could be especially perverse about all this: challenging, provoking, and yet, in spite of his radical intentions, somewhat appeasing in his emphases' (Bersani, 2010, p.26).

60 See the previous note.

61 A more articulated and extended formulation of this 'addition' can be found in the fifth chapter of my book, *Queer Apocalypses: Elements of Antisocial Theory* (2017).

62 'But is it really possible for anyone seriously interested in Foucault on fantasy, sexuality, and power not to engage him in a confrontation with psychoanalysis? Can anyone believe that such peremptory formulas as *l'Art de vivre c'est de tuer la psychologie* make any sense except as an aggressive riposte to an interlocutor Foucault seldom acknowledges or addresses directly? He was so acutely aware of psychoanalysis as yet another episode in a history of disciplinary networks that he never considered that psychoanalysis might provide some answers to questions he himself found urgent' (Bersani, 1995, pp.97–98).

63 'As I have been using the term, *jouissance* refers to a "erotogenicity" that, in the *Three Essays*, Freud (1905/2017) ascribes not only to the body's entire surface and all the internal organs, but also to any activities and mental states or affective processes (he mentions

intellectual strain, wrestling, railway travel) that produce a certain degree of intensity in the organism and in so doing momentarily disturb psychic organization. Following Jean Laplanche, who speaks of the sexual as an effect of *ébranlement*, I call jouissance "self-shattering" in that it disrupts the ego's coherence and dissolves its boundaries' (Bersani, 1995, p.101).

64 Bersani takes into account Foucault's thesis on sadomasochism especially in the third chapter of *Homos*, titled 'The Gay Daddy'.

65 'Women and gay men spread their legs with an unquenchable appetite for destruction' (Bersani, 2010, p.18).

66 In equestrian parlance, 'bareback' indicates the activity of riding without saddle. By extension, since the mid-1990s in gay circles in major American cities, the term has come to mean the search for unprotected anal sex in order to deliberately become HIV positive. In the second chapter of *Intimacies*, titled 'Shame on You', published with some revisions in Halley and Parker's *After Sex: On Writing Since Queer Theory* (2011), Bersani refers to Tim Dean's ethnographic research on the subject *Unlimited Intimacy: Reflections on the Subculture of Barebacking* (2009), to condemn this practice, which he nonetheless interprets as a form of ascetic spirituality aimed at challenging the centrality of the self, and at the dissolution of personality, as a 'a ritual of sacrificial love' (Bersani, 2011, p.105). According to Bersani, 'bug-chasing and gift-giving [is a] sexually repellent and staggeringly irresponsible behavior' (2011, p.105). This judgement leads him to rethink the argument contained in 'Is the Rectum a Grave?' to point out that the 'principal interest of a self-shattering sexuality was [fundamentally] its moral value' (p.107) and is based on the 'crucial psychoanalytic distinction between fantasy and reality' (p.107). In this way, Bersani refers to concepts such as 'pleasure' and 'self-preservation' that he would once have attributed to the liberal conception of the subject and re-evaluates Foucault's thought: 'I now see something both naïve and dangerous in this claim. While I continue to believe that, following a cue given to us by Foucault, a certain training in forms of self-divestiture is a politically and morally imperative ascesis, any such training has to be the psychic condition of possibility rather than the praxis of, to quote Foucault, "new relational modes". Barebacking is a literalizing of the ontology of the sexual. As such, it also implicitly destroys the crucial psychoanalytic distinction between fantasy and reality—or to specify this necessary but by now banal opposition, between the unbounded potentiality of the unconscious and the at times tragically limited consequentiality of what is realized, of what *is*. "Is the Rectum a Grave?" celebrates the rectum as the grave of phallic power; barebacking celebrates the rectum as the grave *tout court* … [W]e have to say that barebacking answers the title of my 1987 essay with a definitive yes. If that affirmation repels us, it should lead to a rethinking of self-divestiture, one in which potentially catastrophic self-shattering is replaced by an ego at once self-divesting and self-disseminating. Ego

identity, the individual personality, could then be sacrificed not to biological or psychic death but, rather, to the pleasure of finding multiple parts of ourselves inaccurately replicated everywhere in the world. This would be the pleasure of what Adam Phillips and I call impersonal narcissism' (Bersani, 2011, pp.107–108).

67 This opinion is also found in Preciado (2013) *Testo Junkie*, where Preciado labels 'Guy Hocquenghem, René Scherer and Monique Wittig', as the 'early French queer theorists' (p.335, footnote 2).

68 Preciado (2018) states: 'Roland Barthes, for whom it was more difficult to talk about his homosexuality in public than to do hermeneutics, invented in 1971 a category without knowing that it would be the most appropriate one to qualify the book that Guy Hocquenghem would write a year later: textual terrorism. By referring to Sade, Fourier and Loyola's work Barthes calls terrorist those texts capable of "social intervention", not because of their popularity or success, but thanks to the "violence that allows the text to exceed the laws that a society, an ideology, or a philosophy establish in order to build its own historical intelligibility". Hocquenghem's *Le Désir homosexuel* is not simply one book on homosexuality. It is the first terrorist text that directly addresses hegemonic heterosexual language. It is the first critical-diagnostic text on the relationship between capitalism and heterosexuality written by a fag who does not hide his condition of "social scum" and "weird" person to begin to speak' (p.23). Barthes quotation comes from Barthes (1972, p.14) *Sade, Fourier, Loyola*.

69 In addition to the already quoted essays included in the journal *PMLA*, issue 3, 2006 (see Caserio et al., 2006), see de Lauretis (2008) and Halberstam (2011).

70 In the last pages of Book II of his Seminar, *The Ego in Freud's Theory and in the Technique of Psychoanalysis* (1978/1998) dedicated to the concept of 'ego', Lacan argues that the price that human beings pay to have access to the symbolic order, that is, to language and the law, is the loss of the real. For the speaking subject the real can in fact be inferred only in mediated form, like the signified to which a signifier alludes. However, the constitution of the speaking subject is not the only effect of the acquisition of language. Along with it, like its obscene Siamese twin, the subject of the drive is born. If the former reacts to the loss of the real with the desire to fill this ontological lack on the level of the imaginary through constructions of meaning, the latter knows no symbols and has the urge to adhere immediately to the real that it has lost. Its modality of existence is jouissance, in which the ego is sucked by the thing (the Freudian Ding) in a vortex that leaves no room for meaning.

71 See Chapter 1, note 1.

72 See notes 4 and 7 in this chapter.

73 The proceedings of the conference are included in 'Queer Bonds', special issue of *GLQ* (Young and Weiner, 2011).

74 See Staiger et al. (2010). Before that, see Sedgwick (2003), Cvetkovich (2003) and Ahmed (2004, 2010).
75 Halberstam refers here to Cvetkovich (2012) and to Love (2007).
76 For Halberstam's own pronoun preferences see www.jackhalberstam. com/on-pronouns/.
77 Beside the texts of the three authors quoted in this book, see the special issue entitled 'Queer Futures' edited by Murphy et al. (2008), and Yekani et al. (2013).
78 In *Queer Apocalypses: Elements of Antisocial Theory* (Bernini, 2017) I define this as apocalyptic temporality.

References

Ahmed, S. (2004) *The Cultural Politics of Emotions*. New York and London: Routledge.

Ahmed, S. (2010) *The Promise of Happiness*. Durham and London: Duke University Press.

Altman, D. (1986) *AIDS in the Mind of America*. New York: Doubleday.

Anzaldùa, G. (1987) *Borderlands/La Frontera: The New Mestiza*. San Francisco: Aunt Lute.

Arietti, L., Ballarin, C., Cuccio, G. and Marcasciano, P. (eds) (2010) *Elementi di critica trans*. Roma: manifestolibri.

Barthes, R. (1972) *Sade, Fourier, Loyola*. Paris: Seuil.

Bernini, L. (2009) 'Riconoscersi umani nel vuoto di Dio. Judith Butler, tra Antigone ed Hegel' in L. Bernini and O. Guaraldo (eds), *Differenza e relazione. L'ontologia dell'umano nel pensiero di Judith Butler e Adriana Cavarero*. Verona: ombre corte, pp.15–38.

Bernini, L. (2016) 'Pollyanna postumana desidera morire. L'eredità di Foucault tra affermatività femminista e negatività queer' in L. Bazzicalupo and S. Vaccaro (eds), *Vita, politica, contingenza*. Macerata: Quodlibet, pp.219–236.

Bernini, L. (2017) *Queer Apocalypses: Elements of Antisocial Theory*. Translated by J. Heim. London and New York: Palgrave Macmillan.

Bersani, L. (1995) *Homos*. Cambridge, MA: Harvard University Press.

Bersani, L. (2010) *Is the Rectum a Grave? And Other Essays*. Chicago and London: The University of Chicago Press.

Bersani, L. (2011) 'Shame on You' in J. Halley and A. Parker (eds), *After Sex: On Writing Since Queer Theory*. Durham, NC: Duke University Press, pp.91–109.

Bersani, L. and Phillips, A. (2008) *Intimacies*. Chicago and London: University of Chicago Press.

Braidotti, R. (2013) *The Posthuman*. Cambridge: Polity Press.

Busarello, R. (2016) 'Diversity management, pinkwashing aziendale e omoneoliberismo. Prospettive critiche sul caso italiano' in F. Zappino (ed.), *Il genere. Tra neoliberismo e neofondamentalismo*. Verona: ombre corte, pp.74–85.

Butler, J. (1999 [1990]) *Gender Trouble: Feminism and the Subversion of Identity*. New York and London: Routledge.

Butler, J. (1993) *Bodies that Matter: On the Discursive Limits of Sex*. New York and London: Routledge.

Butler, J. (2000) *Antigone's Claim: Kinship Between Life and Death*. New York: Columbia University Press.

Butler, J. (2003) *Giving an Account of Oneself: A Critique of Ethical Violence*. Amsterdam: Royal Van Gorcum.

Butler, J. (2004a) *Undoing Gender*. New York and London: Routledge.

Butler, J. (2004b) *Precarious Life: The Powers of Mourning and Violence*. New York and London: Verso.

Butler, J. (2009) *Frames of War: When Is Life Grievable?* New York and London: Verso.

Butler, J. (2015) *Notes Toward a Performative Theory of Assembly*. Cambridge, MA: Harvard University Press.

Caserio, R.L., Edelman, L., Halberstam, J., Muñoz, J.E. and Dean, T.J. (2006) 'The Antisocial Thesis in Queer Theory', *PMLA* 121(3): 819–828.

Cooper, M. (2008) *Life as a Surplus: Biotechnology and Capitalism in the Neoliberal Era*. Seattle and London: University of Washington Press.

Cooper, M. and Waldby, C. (2014) *Clinical Labor: Tissue Donors and Research Subjects in the Global Bioeconomy*. Durham, NC: Duke University Press.

Crenshaw, K. (1989) 'Demarginalizing the Intersection of Race and Sex: A Black Feminist Critique of Antidiscrimination Doctrine, Feminist Theory and Antiracist Politics', *The University of Chicago Legal Forum* 1: 139–167.

Cvetkovich, A. (2003) *An Archive of Feelings: Trauma, Sexuality and Lesbian Public Cultures*. Durham, NC and London: Duke University Press.

Cvetkovich, A. (2012) *Depression: A Public Feeling*. Durham, NC and London: Duke University Press.

De Lauretis, T. (1991) 'Queer Theory: Lesbian and Gay Sexualities: An Introduction', *differences* 3(2): iii–xviii.

De Lauretis, T. (1999) 'La nemesi di Freud. Per un'archeologia degli studi su genere, sessualità e cultura' in T. Lauretis (ed.), *Soggetti eccentrici*. Milano: Feltrinelli, pp.81–118.

De Lauretis, T. (2008) *Freud's Drive: Psychoanalysis, Literature and Film*. London and New York: Palgrave Macmillan.

Dean, T. (2009) *Unlimited Intimacy: Reflections on the Subculture of Barebacking*. Chicago: University of Chicago Press.

Deleuze, G. and Guattari, F. (1972) *Anti-Oedipus: Capitalism and Schizophrenia* 1. Translated by R. Hurley, M. Seem and H.R. Lane (2000). Minneapolis: University of Minnesota Press.

Deleuze, G. and Guattari, F. (1980) *A Thousand Plateaus: Capitalism and Schizophrenia* 2. Translated by B. Massumi (2005). Minneapolis: University of Minnesota Press.

Duggan, L. (2004) *The Twilight of Equality: Neoliberalism, Cultural Politics and the Attack on Democracy*. Boston: Beacon Press.

Edelman, L. (2004) *No Future: Queer Theory and the Death Drive*. Durham, NC and London: Duke University Press.

Ehrenberg, A. (1998) *La Fatigue d'être soi*. Paris: Odile Jacob.

Fanon, F. (1952) *Black Skin, White Masks*. Translated by C.L. Markmann (2008). London: Pluto Press.

Feinberg, L. (1992) *Transgender Liberation: A Movement Whose Time Has Come*. New York: World View Forum.

Feinberg, L. (1997) *Transgender Warriors*. Boston: Beacon Press.

Ferguson, R. (2003) *Aberrations in Black: Toward a Queer of Color Critique*. Minneapolis: University of Minnesota Press.

FHAR (1971) *Rapport contre la normalité*. Paris: Champ libre, coll. Symptome 3.

Foucault, M. (1975) *Discipline and Punish: The Birth of the Prison*. Translated by A. Sheridan (1995). New York: Vintage Books.

Foucault, M. (1976) *The History of Sexuality Volume 1: An Introduction*. Translated by R. Hurley (1978). New York: Pantheon Books.

Foucault, M. (1978) 'Sexuality and Power'. Conference paper given at the University of Tokyo, 20 April 1978. Originally published as 'Sei to kenryoku', *Gendai-shisô*, July 1978, pp.58–77.

Foucault, M. (1997) 'Sex, Power and the Politics of Identity' in P. Rabinow (ed.), *Ethics, Subjectivity and Truth*. Translated by R. Hurley and others. New York: The New Press, pp.163–173.

Foucault, M. (2003a) *Abnormal: Lectures at the College de France 1974–1975*. Translated by G. Burchell. New York: Verso.

Foucault, M. (2003b) *Society Must Be Defended: Lectures at the Collège de France 1975–1976*. Translated by D. Macey. New York: Picador.

Foucault, M. (2006) *Psychiatric Power: Lectures at the Collège de France 1973–1974*. Translated by G. Burchell. London and New York: Palgrave Macmillan.

Foucault, M. (2008) *The Birth of Biopolitics: Lectures at the Collège de France 1978–1979*. Translated by G. Burchell. New York and London: Palgrave Macmillan.

Foucault, M. (2009) *Security, Territory, Population: Lectures at the Collège de France 1977–1978*. Translated by G. Burchell. New York and London: Palgrave Macmillan.

Foucault, M. (2011) 'The Gay Science'. Translated by N. Morar and D.W. Smith, *Critical Inquiry* 37(3): 385–403.

Freud, S. (1905) *Three Essays on the Theory of Sexuality*. Translated by P. Van Haute (2017). London: Verso Books.

Freud, S. (1920) *Beyond the Pleasure Principle*. Translated by J. Strachey (1959). New York: W.W. Norton & Co.

Freud, S. (1921) *Group Psychology and the Analysis of the Ego*. Translated by James Strachey (1959). New York: W.W. Norton & Co.

Freud, S. (1930) *Civilization and Its Discontents*. Translated by D. McLintock (2002). London: Penguin.

Geazry, A.M. (2014) *Antiblack Racism and the AIDS Epidemic*. London and New York: Palgrave Macmillan.

Halberstam, J.J. (2005) *In a Queer Time and Place: Transgender Bodies, Subcultural Lives*. New York: New York University Press.

Halberstam, J.J. (2006) 'The Politics of Negativity in Recent Queer Theory', *PMLA* 3: 823–824.

Halberstam, J.J. (2011) *The Queer Art of Failure*. Durham, NC and London: Duke University Press.

Hocquenghem, G. (1972) *Homosexual Desire*. Translated by D. Dangoor (1993). Durham, NC and London: Duke University Press.

Idier, A. (2007) *Les Vies de Guy Hocquenghem*. Paris: Fayard.

Johnson, E.P. and Henderson, M.G. (eds) (2005) *Black Queer Studies: A Critical Anthology*. Durham, NC and London: Duke University Press.

Kant, I. (2006) 'The Contest of the Faculties, Part 2. The Question Renewed: Is Humankind Continually Improving? [1758]' in P. Kleingeld (ed. and intro.), *Toward Perpetual Peace and Other Writings on Politics, Peace and History*. Translated by D.L. Colclasure. Binghamton: Yale University Press, pp.68–109.

Kristeva, J. (1982) *Powers of Horror: An Essay on Abjection*. New York: Columbia University Press.

Lacan, J. (1978) *The Seminar of Jacques Lacan: Book II. The Ego in Freud's Theory and in the Technique of Psychoanalysis 1954–1955*. Translated by S. Tomaselli (1998). New York and London: Cambridge University Press.

Laplanche, J. (1970) *Life and Death in Psychoanalysis*. Translated by J. Mehlman (1976). Baltimore: Johns Hopkins University Press.

Laplanche, J. (1992) *La Révolution copernicienne inachevée. Travaux 1967–1992*. Paris: Aubier.

Laplanche, J. (2011) *Freud and the Sexual: Essays 2000–2006*. Translated by J. Fletcher, J. House and N. Ray. New York: International Psychoanalytic Books.

Lonzi, C. (1971) 'La donna clitoridea e la donna vaginale' in C. Lonzi, *Sputiamo su Hegel* (2013). Milano: Edizioni, pp.61–113.

Love, H. (2007) *Feeling Backward: Loss and The Politics of Queer History*. Cambridge, MA: Harvard University Press.

Macharia, K. (2013) 'Queer Genealogies (Provisional Notes)', *bullybloggers*, 13(January). Available at: https://bullybloggers.wordpress.com/2013/01/13/queer-genealogies-provisional-notes/ (accessed 31 October 2019).

Marcuse, H. (1955) *Eros and Civilization: A Philosophical Enquiry into Freud*. Boston: Beacon Press.

Marcuse, H. (1964) *One Dimensional Man: Studies in the Ideology of Advanced Industrial Society*. Boston: Beacon Press.

Marshall, B. (1997) *Guy Hocquenghem: Beyond Gay Identity*. Durham, NC: Duke University Press.

Marzano, M. (2015) *Papà, mamma e gender*. Turin: UTET.

Massad, J.A. (2007) *Desiring Arabs*. Chicago: University of Chicago Press.

Mieli, M. (1977) *Towards a Gay Communism: Elements of a Homosexual Critique*. Translated by D. Fernbach and E. Calder Williams (2018). London: Pluto Press.

Moraga, C. (1983) *Loving in the War Years*. Boston: South End Press.

Muñoz, J.E. (1999) *Disidentification: Queers of Color and the Performance of Politics*. Minneapolis: University of Minnesota Press.

Muñoz, J.E. (2006) 'Thinking Beyond Anti Relationality and Anti Utopianism in Queer Critique', *PMLA* 3: 825–826.

Muñoz, J.E. (2009) *Cruising Utopia: The There and Then of Queer Futurity*. New York: New York University Press.

Murphy, K., Ruiz, J. and Serlin, D. (eds) (2008) 'Queer Futures', *Radical History Review* 100.

Oliverio, S., Sicca, L.M. and Valerio, P. (eds) (2016) *Trasformare le pratiche nelle organizzazioni di lavoro e di pensiero*. Napoli: Editoriale Scientifica.

Pateman, C. (1988) *The Sexual Contract*. Cambridge: Polity Press.

Penney, J. (2013) *After Queer Theory*. London: Pluto Press.

Prearo, M. (2014) *Le Moment politique de l'homosexualité. Mouvements, identités et communautés en France*. Lyon: Presses universitaires de Lyon.

Prearo, M. (2015) *La fabbrica dell'orgoglio. Una genealogia dei movimenti LGBT*. Pisa: Edizioni ETS.

Preciado, P.B. (2009) 'Terror anal' in G. Hocquenghem, *El deseo homosexual*. Barcelona: Melusina, pp.133–172.

Preciado, P.B. (2013) *Testo Junkie: Sex, Drugs and Biopolitics in the Pharmaco-Pornographic Era*. Translated by B. Benderson. New York: The Feminist Press.

Preciado, P.B. (2014) *Pornotopia: An Essay on Playboy's Architecture and Biopolitics*. Cambridge, MA: MIT Press.

Preciado, P.B. (2018) *Terrore anale. Appunti sui primi giorni della rivoluzione sessuale*. Translated by ideadestroyingmuros. Milano: Fandango.

Puar, J. (2007) *Terrorist Assemblages: Homonationalism in Queer Times*. Durham, NC: Duke University Press.

Quaranta, P. (2004) 'Nel nome di Pan', *Babilonia* 228(February): 46–49.

Rao, R. (2010) *Third World Protest: Between Home and the World*. Oxford and New York: Oxford University Press.

Reich, W. (1942) *The Function of the Orgasm: Sex Economic Problems of Biological Energy*. Translated by V.R. Carfagno (1973). New York: Farrar Strauss and Giroux.

Reich, W. (1936) *The Sexual Revolution: Towards a Sex Regulating Character Structure*. Translated by T. Pol (1974). New York: Farrar Strauss and Giroux.

Rich, A. (1980) 'Compulsory Heterosexuality and Lesbian Existence', *Signs* 5(4): 631–660.

Rifkin, M. (2011) *When Did Indians Become Straight? Kinship, The History of Sexuality, and Native Sovereignty*. Oxford and New York: Oxford University Press.

Sedgwick (Kosofsky), E. (1990) *Epistemology of the Closet*. Berkeley: University of California Press.

Sedgwick (Kosofsky), E. (1994) *Tendencies*. New York and London: Routledge.

Sedgwick (Kosofsky), E. (2003) *Touching Feeling: Affect, Pedagogy, Performativity*. Durham, NC and London: Duke University Press.

Shah, N. (2012) *Stranger Intimacy: Contesting Race, Sexuality and the Law in the North American West*. Oakland: University of California Press.

Sharpe, C. (2010) *Monstruous Intimacies: Making Post-Slavery Subjects*. Durham, NC and London: Duke University Press.

Sneadiker, D.M. (2009) *Queer Optimism: Lyric Personhood and Other Felicitous Persuasions*. Minneapolis: University of Minnesota Press.

Spillers, H. (1987) 'Mama's Baby, Papa's Maybe: An American Grammar Book', *Diacritics* 17(2): 64–81.

Staiger, J., Cvetkovich, A. and Reynolds, A. (eds) (2010) *Political Emotions*. New York and London: Routledge.

Stryker, S. (2008) 'Transgender History, Homonormativity, and Disciplinarity', *Radical History Review* 10: 144–157.

Stryker, S. and Dierkes-Thrun, P. (2014) 'Transgender Studies Today: An Interview with Susan Stryker', *Boundary online* 2. Available at www. boundary2.org/2014/08/transgender-studies-today-an-interview-with-susan-stryker/ (accessed 4 November 2019).

Warner, M. (ed.) (1993) *Fear of a Queer Planet: Queer Politics and Social Theory*. Minneapolis: University of Minnesota Press.

Warner, M. (ed.) (1999) 'Normal and Normaller: Beyond Gay Marriage', *GLQ* 5(2): 119–171.

Watney, S. (1987) 'The Spectacle of Aids', *October* 43(Winter): 71–86.

Wittig, M. (1992) *The Straight Mind and Other Essays*. Boston: Beacon Press.

Yekani, E.H., Kilian, E. and Michaelis, B. (eds) (2013) *Queer Futures: Reconsidering Ethics, Activism, and the Political*. New York and London: Routledge.

Young, D. and Weiner, J.J. (eds) (2011) 'Queer Bonds', special issue of *GLQ* 2–3.

Young, I.M. (1990) 'Abjection and Oppression: Dynamic of Unconscious Racism, Sexism and Homophobia' in A.B. Dallery, H. Roberts and C. Scott (eds), *Crises in Continental Philosophy*. Albany: Suny Press, pp.201–213.

Zappino, F. (2016) *Il genere. Tra neoliberismo e neofondamentalismo*. Verona: ombre corte.

Index

For Product Safety Concerns and Information please contact our EU
representative GPSR@taylorandfrancis.com
Taylor & Francis Verlag GmbH, Kaufingerstraße 24, 80331 München, Germany

www.ingramcontent.com/pod-product-compliance
Lightning Source LLC
Chambersburg PA
CBHW050517280326
41932CB00014B/2354